I Expected to be Fired

Jen Southworth

WINEPRESS WP PUBLISHING

Printed in the United States of America

Packaged by WinePress Publishing, PO Box 1406, Mukilteo, WA 98275. The views expressed or implied in this work do not necessarily reflect those of WinePress Publishing. Ultimate design, content, and editorial accuracy of this work is the responsibility of the author(s).

ISBN 1-57921-126-7
Library of Congress Catalog Card Number: 98-60795

This book is dedicated to my husband, our son, and the many friends in the Pacific Northwest who urged me to write these incidents. I am particularly grateful to those who gave me permission to write what I remember concerning them. Their real names appear. Reader, if you recall any of these events but the names are wrong, you are right. I took the liberty to change those names because I do not want to embarrass anyone. The Paks are the only people whose correct name is used without their permission. They went back to Korea. They wanted their own doctor to treat an ugly growth Kumjah had developed. None of the author's sources could locate their Korean address.

I am very grateful to Paula Craig and Sherry Larson, my recorders; especially to Fran T. Starrett, the cartoon artist; as well as friends who made suggestions when the copy wasn't clear: Don Jones, Jean Whitford, Edna Smith, Jan Dillan, and Marilyn Bennett.

Table of Contents

Part Three: Pleasure

Foreword

R eading stories about a truly dedicated teacher is ageless. Jen Southworth is ageless, continuing to help adults learn to read through her involvement after retirement in the community Literacy Council.

She is the epitome of what a high-school teacher should be in education—a totally committed professional in all aspects of her teaching.

Characteristics that contributed to her outstanding performance were as follows: high educational expectations and standards; a sense of humor; a caring attitude towards her students; and the ability to communicate with students, parents, and fellow staff members.

In closing, comments by Bill Moyer in a AASA speech in 1976 personify Jen Southworth, "A student and a teacher cross paths once and something eternal is born that in the deepest gloom and despair of a cynical age affirms the steadfastness of the human heart and inevitable triumph of the human soul."

HARRY L. GUAY, PH. D.
Former Assistant Superintendent
Central School District

---

* AUTHOR'S NOTE: Dr. Guay was one of the district administrators who could have fired the author.

Part One

Chapter 1

Preparation

It was Christmas Eve 1928. Although I had been teaching Sunday school for some time, this was my first directing of something resembling a dramatic production. The Beginners were first on the program in the little prairie church. Nine kiddos, ranging from four to six years—each clutching a big capital letter to spell C-H-R-I-S-T-M-A-S—were standing still (for them). Lottie was seven going on eight. She had never been in a program. Everyone knew she was tongue-tied. Her face and her mother's both lit up when she was assigned this "piece":

Merry Christmas, girls and boys,
We wish you this with deep joy!

The bedsheet curtain pulled open. Lottie walked straight to the middle of the raised platform, smiled, and said:

May-ee Kit-tum due 'm boy
Ee ish you di wi deepum joe.

Lottie's mother was seated on the middle aisle next to Lottie's father. He sat beside my father, who sat next to my mother. She was practically on the wall. In the loudest stage whisper ever, Lottie's mother said, "Wasn't 'at wunnerful? You could 'unnerstan' every word!"

Thereupon my irreligious father whispered in my mother's ear, "Lottie's ma is 'better'n Jesus Christ. God Himself couldn't understand that kid."

Sixty-two years later, the memory of Lottie's piece caused me to laugh hilariously. But of that later.

In the late 1930s, my schedule at State College included two classes in practice teaching. Pacific Northwest colleges and universities grant credit for the same classes but designate them *cadet teaching* or *practicum*.

The first class was sophomore English in the college's Practice High School. The other was in a parochial school almost a couple miles from the college campus. That was thirty years before I became a Christian.

Belle Curvertino, my English supervisor, had a large protruding abdomen, emphasized by the current fashion of tightly fitting knitted dresses. My boyfriend and I thought she was seeing his father, a book salesman, more than she should. Constantly, so it seemed, Mrs. Curvertino quizzed me about my boyfriend's family. This was welcome respite from her usual pouncing on me like two seagulls on one clam. Now, years later, after having had several cadet teachers to supervise in a public high school, I can understand her pouncing, but not her lack of tact. Then, I resented her.

One bright sophomore girl in the Practice High School didn't have much love for the "super" either. They had tangled before. On the day Mary Ellen, the student, chose to give an expository speech, she appeared in her mother's knitted dress and high-heeled shoes. I thought she probably had an early dismissal slip because her clothing was so different from her usual sweater, dirndl skirt, and rubber-heeled brown oxfords.

When called upon, Mary Ellen marched up to the chalkboard, planted her feet far apart, and began to write a column of figures and letters. She explained the normal curve of grading. At the culmination of her talk, she turned sideways and sticking out her tummy as far as possible, she said, "This is the Belle curve!"

At that moment, three things happened: First, the other thirty-plus students started to roar. Second, my knee bent and I felt a run starting in my new thirty-nine-cent rayon stocking. "D@!*," escaped my lips. Third, Mrs. Curvertino walked in the door!

Mary Ellen's face blanched as she saw Belle Curvertino. Then, with head down, she sped to her seat. Silence was deadening. Praise the Lord, the dismissal bell rang and Mrs. Curvertino left.

To this day I don't know how much the supervisor heard, but I was shaken. Fifty years ago Education Departments—yes, even high schools—frowned on slang. Profanity was an absolute no-no. Physical punishment, however, was not only condoned but also encouraged when all else failed. What a contrast to the days since my retirement!

Spring quarter my practice-teaching class in vocal music was in Sacred Heart Academy. Since the academy was almost two miles distant from my dorm, I thought I could walk faster to it than the streetcar and bus transfers could get me there. My college music supervisor had told me that I was to be at the Academy for their fifth period, which to me was 2:30 P.M. To the Academy, that was 2:00 P.M. Murphy's Law took over.

Thinking I would arrive early, I got there almost half an hour late. Walks had not been shoveled in the sparsely inhabited area on the outskirts of the city, but there were no street lights or traffic. Only six inches of snow impeded me.

Blessed old Mother Mary Kate welcomed me with a smile, a hot cup of coffee, and two oatmeal cookies. She refused to share them with me. In her faint Irish brogue she said, "We arre keeping Lint, ya know."

"We cun a-joost your toim as needed, Miss, with your college toim," she added as I apologized.

Hobbling on badly bunioned feet, she led me to the music room. It held all fifty-some of the four-year student body. A couple were beating out "Chopsticks" on a beautiful, ebony grand piano. A foot steadily held the right-hand pedal down in the attempt to drown out the noise the rest of the kids were making. Mother Superior clapped her arthritic hands—her fingertips were at least two inches apart, but her palms connected.

"Children, children," her sweet voice called several times as she hobbled about the room on her sore bunions. At each call of "Children, children" more giggling students joined the conga line behind her.

At last Mother's calls turned to cries. *How could those insensitive monsters treat that sweet old lady like that?* I wondered. *They won't do that to me!* By now all fifty-two kids had joined in the fun and Mother Mary Kate's red face was panting. I could stand it no longer.

"Stop it!" I roared in decibels exceeding the stomping and giggling. All action stopped. Between gasps Mother Mary Kate briefly introduced me and hobbled out. The door banged behind her. Half a century later I know I was just as insensitive to Mother's feelings as her students. All I felt then was triumph.

It was short-lived. I was standing in the curve of that beautiful piano. A big hulk, the biggest senior boy, thinking he was God's gift to young females, quickly lifted me by the armpits and deposited me *on* the piano.

"Would you do this to Mother Mary Kate?" I demanded.

"No. She doesn't look like you or wear clothes like you." He smiled with enjoyment.

Squeezing my chin between his thumb and finger, he brought my head back and his face close to mine. Thanks to my childhood—four boy cousins, three of them older than I—I had learned to defend myself. He got the back of my right hand on his right cheek and the palm on the other side of his face with an even harder slap.

"Now," I said, with as much dignity as I could muster while sliding off the piano and dusting my hands, "we'll all get to work."

That led to testing voices with scales on the piano. The students obeyed to the letter, writing their names under the lists of alto, soprano, tenor, or bass as I designated. Mother Mary Kate came in hours later to say school was out. She was astonished! The room was quiet except for the last student's climbing the soprano scale. Astonished, too, to learn all girls couldn't sing soprano and all boys couldn't sing alto, as she had been trying to do with the anthem.

I can't remember why I missed the students' final production of "The Heavens Resound." My two days a week with the kids for the quarter were in preparation for the Bishop's Silver Jubilee.

Mother Mary Kate told me as soon as possible: "The Bishop was *so* pleased. He said they behaved and sounded like angels!" Then she added, "Their harmony was truly heavenly, and they were so easy to direct."

My credits came through that June as follows: Practice Teaching—English, 5 hours, A; Practice Teaching—Vocal Music, 2 hours, A+.

❧   ❧   ❧

The good Lord has let me live long enough to learn that He prepares one in advance for challenges to come. During the fall of 1937, He prepared me for physical combat in my first school.

My senior year in state college, I worked for my board waiting on the counter and tables in a little combination deli and restaurant. It was across the street from the women's dorm. The job consisted of working during breakfast, lunch, and dinner, five days a week. Saturdays, I worked four to five hours washing woodwork, windows, and walls. Natural gas, from the cooking in the kitchen to heating the rest of the building, coated white enameled walls and fixtures with greasy black.

On the second Saturday, Bill, the owner's son, hit me between the shoulders. It was the first time the sixteen-year-old had seen me.

"Kick off your spike heels and stand flat-footed, as tall as you can," he directed.

He stood back-to-back with me and measured our tousled heads with his hand.

"You're five even; so am I," he said. Then he added, "How much do you weigh?"

"The scale fluctuates between ninety-five and ninety-eight pounds," I replied.

"Hold out your arm," he demanded, while placing his arm beside mine. "You're *perfect!*" he shouted.

Perfect for what? I wondered. Perfect for his punching bag because we were the same size, and he was training for the Golden Gloves. (The next year he was champion in his division in the final tournament in Minneapolis.) From our first meeting, he made my Saturdays miserable.

One weekend Bill Sr. sent Bill Jr. on a long errand. It seems the father thought his son had interfered enough with my work. My employer put Bill Jr.'s boxing gloves on me and gave me a golden lesson. Bill Sr. was a retired pro boxer. His lesson paid off. The next week, Bill Jr. brought out the gloves and was surprised that I countered all his blows. Not too long after that, he quit begging me to spar. Why? I had knocked him to his knees.

Little did I know what preparation the two Bills had given me for my first year of teaching in one tough, small-town school. The year before, the students had thrown out three women teachers— one bodily through the window.

Two weeks before school started, some students set fire to the schoolhouse. It burned to the ground. Because it was still during the Great Depression, some citizens despaired. But thanks to an undaunted school board, school started the day after Labor Day as scheduled.

The first three grades started in the basement of a church where they used the Sunday school's small tables and chairs. The rest of us started in an abandoned IGA grocery store on Main Street.

The large store had been hastily divided into four equal rooms, with a cubicle enclosing the store's vault for the principal's office. Three grades—fourth, fifth, and sixth—occupied a back, west room. The front housed the seventh and eighth grades. The four-year high school luxuriated in the two east rooms. The principal taught math and science in the back room close to his office. I tried to teach in the front room. My contract for $720 a year declared me the vice principal.

Although school started on time, it was two weeks before chalkboards, desks, and books arrived. There were benches for students but no seating for the teacher. (No wonder I became a stand-up teacher for thirty-five years!) There wasn't so much as a card table for a desk. I put my own books, papers, etc. on the 1½-by-3-foot ledge inside the wide storefront window.

Most distractions the first days were townspeople pressing their faces and hands against that window. They were trying to see the new, single "school marm." They probably wagered how long I would stay.

Bless her heart, the woman school-board president bought, made, and installed six-foot-long, unbleached muslin curtains on the storefront windows. Those curtains were a godsend on that hot, Midwestern Indian summer. Before equipment, books, and furniture arrived, my three English classes, two history classes, and one vocal music class had to do a lot of writing (on their knees) from dictation.

One hot day, tall, lanky John had enough writing and me. He got up, grabbed my *Collegiate Dictionary* from the window ledge, and threw it at me. Whether from inability or design, the dictionary missed. It landed on the floor with a broken back and a few missing pages. I asked him to pick it up and hand it to me.

Instead, John came at me shouting curses and obscenities, with clenched fists. Thanks to Bill Sr.'s lesson, my body reacted. John had left his face open. My right fist connected with the button on his chin. The blow decked him! Ham actress that I am, I dusted my hands together and asked, "Next?"

There were no takers. Apparently, no one saw my knocking knees beneath my long, very full skirt.

What did I learn? Several things:

1. Never let a teenager know you are afraid of him, her, or the situation.
2. Always do your best with what you have.
3. Each student is worth the teacher's best performance! It is my firm belief that teachers should be worthy role models for their students—or, at least, try to be.

Part Two
Paycheck

Chapter 2
Discipline

My next school was in the Old West. Before my time, the city of about 2,500 had marked the division of territory between cattlemen and sheepherders. Having come from the Midwest, I knew prairie to be slightly rolling hills covered with lush green grass from the black fertile soil. The railway schedule said my new home would be next.

The locomotive jolted each passenger car to a halt. I was ready with my luggage. The door opened. There was *nothing* in sight but bare, reddish-brown, flat ground stretching to beige buttes in the distance. I drew a deep breath, picked up my bags, and was almost off into that vast perpetuity of wind and space. The conductor yelled: "What are you doing, Miss?" Miss—I almost did. The train had stopped at the water tower about three miles out of town.

The good Lord knew all along that I am a better disciplinarian than teacher. Probably because I worked harder on discipline than on teaching. He also knew my English was far superior to my math. When I was a child, my parents and teachers often said, "Jennie was a fairly bright little girl, but she would never learn arithmetic." Jennie believed them—and didn't try—until she was forced to teach math. What a pity she believed the misjudgers. Math is so logical and simple, once the fundamentals are grasped.

Until *that* Monday, administration, faculty, and students did their best to impress upon me what an especially good teacher I had replaced. Two weeks previous, the assignment in eighth-grade English was short. The paper had been due the following Wednesday. Students had had one week and two days to do a one-page, one-resource research paper on a topic of the student's choice. Only one girl of the thirty-six students handed in her paper on time.

"You will all have your papers ready by Monday. Two weeks is sufficient time for a one-source, one-page research paper," said I. There were several snickers. "All papers will be in Monday, or else!" The bell stopped my threats.

That Monday came, but only two papers arrived with it. After dismissing to the library the three students who had completed the assignment, I hurried to the office. Mr. Temple, the principal, gave me the paddle. It had never occurred to me that ten whacks per thirty-three seats would be well over three hundred! My right arm gave up at the fifteenth student. Then my left arm refused to lift the paddle. Mr. Temple was grinning through the glass in the door. He did not enter. The right arm, rested somewhat in the left-handed interim, was able to finish the remaining seats of the thirty-three. Not only were thirty-three papers on my desk Tuesday, but five were in before 9:00 A.M., when the class started.

One week later, the president of the school board visited me right after school.

"Did you paddle my Thomas last week?"

"Yes ma'am," I answered, expecting the worst—to be fired.

"Good!" she exclaimed. "His father is gone for a month. Thomas did something last night that his father would have used the razor strap on him if he had been home. Will you paddle him for me? I have a bad heart condition. Thomas knows I can't deliver physical punishment, but he really needs it."

Mr. Temple confirmed her story and brought me the paddle.

"Why didn't she ask you?" I wanted to know as I returned the paddle following her departure.

"Because I know what Tommy did. As a friend of his father, I'd probably have broken a few bones. It was so bad his mother didn't want you to know what the kid had done."

That's the only physical punishment I ever inflicted without knowing—at least in part—the offense.

Not long after that, Mr. Temple came to my room and laid the keys to his car on my desk.

"Miss Barton, will you drive the junior-high cheerleaders to the game this afternoon? Thomas's mother, the *president* of the school board (he emphasized for the benefit of the students), will take your last class and your library period. I was scheduled to drive the cheerleaders, but Tommy's mother and I have an important meeting with a textbook salesman. It is the only chance to get next year's supply of textbooks at discount."

He didn't know my ability to handle a paddle and to handle a car were two, entirely different things. But I kept thinking, *If pioneer women could drive a covered wagon full of a passel of kids over this sagebrush for hundreds of miles, I ought to be able to get to and from the next town on this gravel road.* It was only fifty miles away. We came home victorious—the team and I.

The next year Mr. Temple asked several young, unmarried teachers—including me—for a favor. The seniors had hired a real live band for the Spring Ball. The administration feared the class might go into debt. They encouraged some of the former male graduates to participate. Seniors and faculty hoped there would be enough two-dollar tickets to pay for the band.

My roommate and I were dating former high-school football players. Those three elected me to go with my date, Charles, to the drugstore to meet the former team's fullback. Then I was to introduce him to Thylda, another teacher. When I first shook hands with Walt (a daring gesture back in "them days"), I thought, *Lucky Thylda.* Walt was a dapper, well-groomed young man. He knew how to smile. His face lit up at first sight. So did mine.

The great night arrived. I had but two formals. No time lost in choosing the one for spring. Charles arrived. I was aghast! To use his own words, he was "all duded up."

He wore a medium light brown, green-and-black checkered Western suit; new buckskin cowboy boots—sans spurs; a maroon

Western shirt with silver trim and pearl buttons; and a bright yellow tie with white polka dots, tied in a big knot under his chin.

Charles was fun, but he stomped like he was killing rattlesnakes at each corner of the gym. He knew many local gals. Consequently, Walt danced with me more than Thylda. His reason: She sang high soprano in his ear. I kept my mouth shut and enjoyed the Senior Ball of 1939.

One year and one week later, Walt slipped a narrow gold band on the ring finger of my left hand. That act was done in the presence of a pastor and two witnesses. Then several of Walt's friends and many of my students enjoyed dressing Walt in some fat-lady flannel nightgown, cramming me into someone's long johns so Walt could—with great resistance—push me in a wheelbarrow. It was decorated with tin cans trailing as he pushed me down Main Street. The school kids rang cowbells and beat aluminum kettles and pans with huge mixing spoons. That act was known as a *charivari*.

Marriage ended my teaching until World War II. Only after that did the state, which was the first to elect a woman governor, decide it was legal for married women to teach in public schools. Heretofore, the Old West had provided young educated women as decent prospective wives for cowboys and sheepherders. School marms were imported by thriving teacher-agencies. A married woman could homeschool her own children and those of a neighbor "iffen they didn't live too 'fer' away, say, fifteen mile or so." Pearl Harbor changed school law in that state in a hurry. Many male teachers enlisted or were drafted. All certified women were called to the schoolhouses.

World War II brought us to the Pacific Northwest. Most of the local young men from the Old West were shipped to Pacific waters for combat. My sister had been living in the "Apple Capital of the World," so we came farther west to await government orders.

Walt and I were expediters for Kaiser's Shipyard. He was a boilermaker, and I landed with the pipe fitters of Marine Pipe. That continued until the first Friday of the next September.

I took our six-and-a-half-year-old boy to school to register him for the first grade. Unknown to us, the principal had silently followed us down the hall after we had left his office. I was carefully explaining to the lad what the "boys' room" meant, on the way to finding the room to which he had been assigned. I was describing the wonderful storybooks and books about facts he could find right next door, plus how and when he could enter the magic land called Library.

"Mrs. Southworth, you've been a teacher, haven't you?" The principal sounded glad.

"Yes. Does it still show?" I queried.

"Very much so," he continued and, handing me a card, said, "School starts Tuesday, the day after Labor Day. As of now I'm five teachers short. Please go to this address and sign up. I'll call the superintendent's office to await you. It closes in fifteen minutes. Please hurry. I'll see you Tuesday."

Only our boy saw his principal on Tuesday. The main office sent me to a junior-senior high school in a housing project down the hill from the elementary building.

When the war was over, we migrated to the Puget Sound area.

Chapter 3
Challenges

The first year I was at Central High School was a challenge, not only for me, but also for the administration and for the students. Despite his age, one young man fresh from the Navy was in my sophomore English class. When I stated at the beginning of the term the requirements for credit by the end of the semester, he strongly hinted that he would *not* comply. Apparently he loathed book reports. (Now, almost fifty years later, I wonder if he had a genuine reading problem.) But then I announced, "If I ever send a student to the office for disciplinary reasons, that student never comes back to my class. Is that understood?"

Dead silence. Carl, the ex-sailor, sneered. He, his parents, and the principal learned I meant business.

Like the one-reference report in the Old West, I granted a few more days for the slowpokes. Carl had done nothing and told me so with an unprintable oath.

"I'll see about that in the office," he said with another oath.

"If you go, Carl, you can't come back!"

"I'll see about that, too!" The door slammed.

After school the next day, the principal entered my room followed by smirking Carl and both his parents. The ensuing discussion ended with my saying, "If Carl comes back, this serves as my thirty-day notice of resignation. If I can't control the student, either he or I don't belong in the same classroom. I thought I had made that perfectly clear to the administration and to all the students."

The four of them left, but later the principal came back. His pleading availed nothing. I told him, "If he comes back, you'll have my thirty-day notice in writing. I made it in the presence of two witnesses, his parents. That student needs to learn obedience, whether to a teacher or a boss, if he ever hopes to get and hold a job."

The student, not I, left Central High School.

Five or ten years later my husband and I met Carl on the street. I stuck out my hand and asked, "Carl Blanding? How are you?"

Reluctantly, he grasped my hand and said, "I thought you hated me and never wanted to see me again."

"No, Carl, it wasn't you. It was what you were *not* doing that I disliked." Then I introduced him to Walt.

"You know, Mr. Southworth, that was the best thing your wife could have done for me. Until then, I thought the Navy was picking on me. For the first time in my life, I realized I had to do what I was told whether I liked it or not if I was going to get and hold a job."

He was then gainfully employed and looked prosperous. Not only that, but his sisters were excellent cooperators in classes thereafter.

Many years later Hugh, an outstanding musician, couldn't keep his hands quiet in a sophomore literature class. He had his book open on his desk directly in front of me. He was beating time to the cadence of the poetry. It must have bothered him that my reading didn't fit the singsong meter he was beating. After I removed the pencil from his hand, he started to slap the desk loudly with his hands in a modern jazz rhythm.

Continuing to read, I covered his hands with my right, free hand. He drew his hands from under mine and slapped my hand. I covered his with more force. He slapped me again, harder. I retaliated with equal strength. He jumped up and ran into the hall. I ran after him. He was so surprised that all he could do was ask, "Whadda yah want me to do?"

"Come back in and sit in your seat *quietly* until the bell rings."

He came and sat, but when the bell rang he was off like a shot to the office. It was noon. En route to the lunch room, I stopped in the counselor's office and got his file from the junior high.

That document revealed that for three years Hugh had established a behavior pattern that plainly said he did not like women teachers. For three years before entering Central High, this had been his pattern: He would be in a woman's class for two weeks; then he would misbehave and be sent to the office. The principal would suspend him for another two weeks. Returning to school, he would enter a different teacher's classroom. If the teacher was another woman, he would stay for two weeks before being suspended again. If the next teacher were a man, Hugh would remain.

The principal called to me as I emerged from the counselor's office. He told me that he had already suspended Hugh for two weeks.

"When he returns, I want him back," I said firmly.

"Are you crazy? By the way, how hard did you hit him?"

"Are you a brave man?" I asked.

"I think so," he replied.

"Put your hands palm down on your desk, and I'll show you." He did and I did. At least I tried to.

"Why so hard?"

"It was in retaliation for the two times he slapped my hand with increasing force."

To this day, I don't know if Hugh had told of slapping my hand or why he had. Then I showed him Hugh's file from the junior high and told the principal it was time that boy learned to do things that he didn't like to do, plus behave himself in a woman's class. Getting out of school for two weeks was really what Hugh wanted, so he could fool around with his musical instrument to his heart's content. No wonder he won state honors as soloist in our jazz band.

The suspension happened in October. Hugh came back and sat next to my desk. He didn't protest. The last day of school before Christmas vacation, he waited until all the rest of the students were gone. Then he said, "Mrs. Souseworse." (He had never learned to pronounce *th*'s.) "I want to wish you an especially Happy Christmas and a Merry New Year!"

He was nervous. He extended a sweaty palm, which was sticky from the Christmas treats the class had shared. I shook it warmly and wished him a joyous holiday, too.

He left. Then I locked the door, went back into the room, and fell on my knees by the closest student desk. With tears streaming down my face, I said loudly, "Thanks, God, for helping me win this kid."

Truly, He had. Besides being a helpful cooperator in class, every time Hugh saw me on campus he would smile broadly and shout for all to hear, "Hi, Mrs. Souseworse. You're my favorite English teacher."

👑   👑   👑

Esmeralda was a big black sophomore girl bent on having her own way, regardless of what it cost others. Most of the time her language and behavior were just shy of being obnoxious. She had natural learning ability and had no time for slow learners, regardless of their color. She had less time for anyone who crossed her.

The counselors had too many sophomores to test them in the study hall as they had formerly done. They revamped the schedule. All tenth-grade classes would be scheduled for two-hour blocks of time for two days. That arrangement would permit English teachers to administer the California Mental Maturity Test in their classrooms. Other teachers and students were duly warned several times in advance.

The test directions for the monitor to read to the testees clearly stated:

> Students who finish early should reread the questions and their answers before the Monitor collects the papers. The students shall remain quietly in their seats until the signal for the short break. Test papers will be collected by the Monitor just before. After the break, a new set of questions will be distributed.

Esmeralda finished a good twenty minutes early. It took her less than three minutes to reread her paper. I went to collect it. Before I could get to her desk, she rose, stretched, and yawning very audibly said, "Whatsa' mattah wit chew guys? You ain't finished?"

Her eyes fell on me. She continued.

"You little white rag of a teachuh, git outta' my way!"

She raised her right arm. I grabbed her wrist with my right hand. The twist-back surprised her as much as my presence. She sank into her seat.

"You git yo' white rag of a face outta' mine!" she bellowed.

Again she was surprised. I gripped her wrist tighter, and calmly but firmly said, "Esmeralda, you will sit *quietly* until the bell, so others can finish. If you make one sound with your mouth or body before that time, you shall not be able to stand or speak until the end of the second session of the test. Do you understand?"

We were eyeball to eyeball. Her black eyes acquiesced, "Yes."

That bold encounter paid off. Not only did Esmeralda behave well the rest of the year, but it also made an impression on her younger sister and her sister's class the following year.

Because Central School District contained several housing projects for several military groups, many students had been shunted from school to school across the nation. Some had even been in US government schools in many parts of the globe. No wonder some became belligerent trying to survive the "zillions" of teachers in required basic subjects. Many of them saw no need for English. They had been speaking American slanguage all their lives. Military rules they respected; English books and school rules were written to be broken.

❄   ❄   ❄

Angelina's behavior plainly stated her belief about rules. Her hair was a burning bush of gold. But her thick glasses and typical adolescent skin must have created a poor self-image in her eyes. She craved attention. She got it, but in the wrong way.

One time she did something more obnoxious than usual. Because the whole class thought her acts and sayings were great sport, I proclaimed, "That's enough! All of you will remain in your seats when the dismissal bell rings. Angelina will remain longer."

"Listen up, you guys!" loudly volunteered Esmeralda's sister. "Miz Southworth mean wot she say. She keep yo' to Ju'ly fo'th iffen you doan shut up an' do whot she asts!"

Even Angelina listened. Her behavior greatly improved. Two days after Reports to Parents were mailed, a smiling Angelina came in before school to lay hers on my desk.

"Please read it," she said.

On the back of the Report to Parents her mother had written of her delight to receive a good behavior report for the first time on "Angie." She wanted to know what I had done.

"Tell your mother that *you* decided to make her and yourself both proud," was my reply.

From then on Angelina improved her behavior and her grades. Instead of fluctuating between *D* and *F*, her next report card bore a *C*; the next was a *B*. Both mother and daughter were very pleased.

Really, they both owed Esmeralda and her younger sister— not me.

👑　👑　👑

From the late '30s to mid '50s women used scarves to cover their heads. What started as a scarf fad remained because it was practical. Clad in a boxy, gray tweed coat, a pair of green zippered flat shoes, and a matching green nylon scarf, I was about to leave for home via the east exit.

Wham! A junior-high geography book hit my buttocks. Instinctively my toes curled inside my flats to hold me onto the top of three cement steps.

"Oh, my gosh! Mrs. Southworth!" exclaimed the holder of the geography text.

He was the middle of the three Decker boys. Fortunately for him, one of my arms was filled with books; the other he couldn't see (because of the boxy coat) supported a briefcase full of papers. I would have loved to *deck* him! His face turned white at the realization that he had hit a teacher instead of a girl classmate.

"Jim, don't you ever, ever dare to hit any female like that again!" I said with authority.

Knowing he was too stunned to speak, I continued. "If you understand, just nod your head yes."

Still pale, he nodded.

Chapter 4

Students to Whom
I Am Indebted

I and most of my five-thousand-plus students owe a debt of gratitude to the following teenagers—Williametta, Robert, Stan, and Gloria—because each one made me a better teacher.

It began during World War II in Ogden-Meadows. My forty-six students in a ninth-grade block suffered with me from homeroom through language arts, civics, Pacific Northwest history, and (I think) spelling. All students were compelled to eat lunch in their homeroom.

Thinking that half hour would be a good opportunity to get acquainted with students—who came from nearly all of the forty-eight states—I decided to join each table for a week at a time during lunch period. There were eight tables. The first day I sat at a table for the first time, most students were reserved. By the second day, all were relaxed and we had fun. During class time the students were assigned a definite seat at a specific table. Lunchtime was *their* time. They sat with their friends at whatever table the group chose.

There were only five blacks, one from Harlem and the rest from the states in the Deep South. During lunch, they seemed most happy to have a black table all to themselves. Boy, were they noisy gigglers—until the Monday I put my lunch sack on their table. Then they were quiet. Talk about the sound of silence. Even the rest of the other tables were quiet—but not for long. No matter how I tried to get a conversation or a giggle going, the result was the same: stony silence. By lunch on Friday, there were precious few "Yes-m's" and slightly more affirmative and negative head shakes. Praise the Lord! There was one crooked smile.

The smile was Williametta's. She had no control over one side of her body, dragged one foot, and had to use her "good han" and arm to place her paralyzed arm on the table. She was highly intelligent and had an excellent sense of humor. Her handwriting matched her sense of humor, but was painfully slow.

Because my presence at Williametta's table made the rest of them so uncomfortable, I stuck it out with them only that week. Not long after that, which I regarded as my failure, a startling thing happened in the hall right outside my door. It could have been ugly.

Without thinking, I wedged myself between two black boys who held drawn blades.

"Give me that pocketknife!" I demanded of Bo. He froze.

"Billy John, close your razor and give it to me, *now!*" I commanded. Billy John was from my room. Bo was not.

Slowly he did, and laid it gently in my outstretched hand. Bo, seeing his big adversary minding the small but commanding little woman, folded his knife and laid it beside the razor.

"Now go to your homeroom," I said.

Billy John was in his seat when I shut the door. I never checked on Bo. If he wanted his knife back, he could ask for it. Neither reclaimed their property.

Before school was out the next spring, Williametta asked me why I didn't ever eat lunch with "us'uns no mo'." I told her I didn't like to make people uncomfortable—especially while they were eating. Unpleasant circumstances made digestion difficult. I wanted all my kids happy and healthy.

Then she told me how much she had appreciated my not asking about her stroke and what had caused it. "All th'other white folk wanna' know fo'sho'." After a pause she said, "We'uns think yo' not half bad."

Bless her heart; her one sparkling eye; and that white, toothsome, crooked smile! Williametta gave me my first lesson in not getting too personal. She taught me something else: Don't talk about physical maladies one can't help.

❧   ❧   ❧

The second lesson from a student came the first year at my beloved Central High School. Fools rush in where angels fear to tread. You, the reader, know by now I'm no angel. Modern educational psychologists will abhor this episode. For the next twenty-five years I worried about the student's feelings, but I did nothing.

"Wah-bert Wubble-you Wice" as he called himself, was a better-than-average-looking senior and a better than average worker. Unfortunately, no one ever taught him to pronounce correctly the sound of the letter R. Like many teenagers who have a crush on young teachers of the opposite sex, Robert had a crush on me. He wanted to impress me. He did. But not the way he had hoped.

As far back as I can remember, my mother and father had read aloud each evening. Mom read a chapter from the King James Version of the Bible. Then Dad read an act of one of Shakespeare's plays. I sat in the reader's lap and turned pages until I was able to read alternating speeches with my father. In his youth, he had traveled with Ringling Brothers Circus and was not a bad actor. He read with imagination and feeling. Small wonder my parents had bred in me a love for the beautiful English language of the 1600s. No such love existed for Robert.

The curriculum guide from the state superintendent of Public Instruction was specific: "Let students choose characters and read a few scenes of *Macbeth* before assigning written questions from their texts." That first year I did that for two days.

Robert had looked for the character with the fewest lines in act 2, scene 3. It was McDuff. He read in a loud staccato monotone, ending the last word on the same pitch as the first. When he came to the discovery of Duncan's death, he read slowly—oh, so slowly: "Oh, hor-roar, hor-roar, hor-roar . . . " I snatched the book from him and reread the scene as I thought the words indicated. The bell rang. *If this gets to the principal, I'll be fired*, I thought.

Twenty-five years later I apologized to Robert at his class reunion. Grasping my outstretched hand with both of his, he was quick to say, "I never felt bad. I was just so glad I didn't have to read any more of those hard words."

Many high-school students learn to hate the world's best writer, Shakespeare, because they don't understand Elizabethan language. Many teachers don't either. From that day on, I read Shakespeare's plays in their entirety. In American slanguage, I would give a brief synopsis and then read in an established voice for each main character. At the end of the scene, I allowed a time for questions; and at the act's end, there was time for genuine student discussion.

Before I "graduated" with the class of '78, the student body saw cuttings of Shakespeare dramatized by my thespians in the Little Theater. We were even featured in *Dramatics* magazine. At a forty-year class reunion, a man stood up and said, "Mrs. Southworth didn't make me love Shakespeare, but she made him tolerable."

Many other students told me as many times, they enjoyed the class they had been sure they were going to hate.

My thanks to Robert W. Rice for making me a better Shakespearean teacher.

🜲   🜲   🜲

Ten years later, I'd forgotten Williametta's lesson. Summer school taught me a sure-fire method to get students to open up and write. The assignment was to write a three-to-five-paragraph paper on "My Most Enjoyable Experience." Those papers were fun. But not so with the following paper: "My Most Difficult Experience."

Stan Tonge, fresh from his parents' divorce, told how hard it was to choose the parent with whom he wanted to live. He developed his topic sentence with logic and clarity. He was determined to stand by his decision. His children would never have to make such a choice.

That was the first and last time I made that assignment. It was too painful and personal for any high-school student, particularly fourteen- and fifteen-year-olds.

❧   ❧   ❧

Because I don't remember her name and have not seen her since her graduation, I shall call her Gloria King. All Christians know what a "King's kid" is. Gloria was certainly one of them. She was also an A+ student.

For my three sophomore English classes I had devised a contract. Belle Curvertino would have been proud of it. Not only did it contain solid literary reading but also some reading from the daily newspaper. The contract allowed students to choose the grade they were willing to attain by doing the required work for it. The C Contract contained the number of stories and their questions from the text that the average student could cover in two weeks. Any questions that were beyond their comprehension (like the one inserted thought question) were discussed in class. The B Contract was half the length of the C Contract, but questions of each day's reading had to be answered with a complete sentence. The A Contract's reading requirement was half the length of the B Contract, but of more difficult material. It required a three-page essay of the student's composition.

Imagine my surprise when Gloria, the best student in the class, handed in a neatly written and errorless C Contract. Astonishment must have sounded in my voice as I inquired, "Why?"

A tear glistened in her eye momentarily; then she said, "I just couldn't do the B Contract and I knew you wouldn't accept the A Contract without the B and C."

"What was wrong with the B Contract?" I asked.

"I just couldn't go against the Bible and read the horoscope diviners and witchcraft," she said quietly but firmly.

"Where did you get that information?" I asked.

"Please, Mrs. Southworth, read the eighteenth chapter of Deuteronomy in the Old Testament of your Bible."

I did, and as a result she and the other sophomores had a choice of comparable reading from other newspaper features. They could stick with the horoscope that term if they chose. But never again.

From then on, I more carefully chose reading material for impressionable teenagers. Thank you, Gloria, for your willingness to sacrifice your grade for your belief. She gave glory to God in her stand as a true King's kid.

Chapter 5
Mistakes

Mistakes were legion. Every one of the thirty-one years at Central High, I expected to be fired. The first year I made the mistake of agreeing to do the makeup for the cast of the Music Department's operetta.

The audience loved it by evidence of several curtain calls. Still, putting away the greasepaint into the makeup box, I found myself lifted up in the arms of the exuberant sophomore tenor. He spun around and around until my spike heel dislodged some plaster from the music room wall.

At that exact moment the principal came through the door. He cleared his throat in his own inimitable way before saying, "Bill, your performance on stage was highly commendable, but I can't say the same for your backstage performance. I will see you in my office first thing Monday morning."

Bill let go of me. Praise the Lord, I had had the presence of mind enough to raise my hands straight above my head. One hand was grasping a stick of greasepaint and the other clutched a rouge pot. Otherwise, the wall would have been marked above the missing plaster.

To me, the principal said nothing. But all weekend I expected to be fired.

🜸 🜸 🜸

No matter where Jim Turner sat, he talked and talked and talked. He was as talkative as I, but I was paid by the school board to talk. After the umpteenth time of having his seat changed, he was still talking.

"Hold out your hand, Jim," I commanded. "You have been warned and moved for the last time."

He raised his fist. I came down hard with the steel edge of a ruler just as he turned and opened his fist.

"Now look what you did!" Jim said loudly.

His palm and under forearm were beet red. That was the last time I ever hit anyone on the palm of the hand with a steel edge— even though Jim had chosen his birthmarked hand to turn and open.

Now, forty years later, Jim raises that hand and his white-bearded face crinkles into a grin when he sees me nearly every day. That greeting happens while we are each mall walking. The mall is less than a mile below the high school where he used to talk and talk.

🜸 🜸 🜸

Report cards were always a pain. Maybe it was my math phobia that made averaging grades purgatory. Maybe it was the constant complaint about low grades. Whatever it was, report cards were painful.

Three examples were not typical. One year Loyal Hamilton was not pleased with the *B* on his first report card from me. He was in senior English class.

"Mrs. Southworth, this is the first *B* I've ever received in my entire life."

"When you've earned an *A* you'll get it," I remarked.

"I don't think you know who I am!"

His tone indicated that his last remark would be the finale to the discussion. But my answer was the finale.

"Loyal, not only do I know you are the school superintendent's son, but I know what your IQ score is. When you put forth the effort to match your ability, you'll get the *A* we both know you are capable of earning."

About ten years later I told his mother about our exchange. That good lady nearly had a fit.

"Why didn't you tell me then?" she asked.

"Because I feared you might kill him," I said.

She replied, "You're right!"

Deep down inside was the real reason: I expected to be fired.

❦   ❦   ❦

A few years after Loyal tried to throw his weight around, Teddy tried.

"What, a *C*? I can't believe my eyes."

"That *C* represents the quality and amount of work you turned in," I countered.

"But athletes don't have time to do all that extra stuff. My dad knows; he was an outstanding football player at the university. He says I have to have at least a *B* in everything if I expect to get into *any* university."

"Teddy, did you make all the touchdowns in last Friday night's game because your father is chairman of the school board?"

"Well . . . no. I caught the passes, saw the holes in the defense, and ran."

"Your father was proud of you, wasn't he?" I asked.

Teddy nodded and grinned.

"Then open your eyes and see what you have to do in *each* class to earn grades to be acceptable to a U. Who knows, you might even get a football scholarship."

Again, I thought, *I might be fired.*

👑   👑   👑

The last one was a genuine big mistake. It was a grade card in drama class. After all the other students left with their report cards, Tom Studeman lingered. He was a real gentleman.

"Mrs. Southworth, I hope you made a mistake on my report card," he said.

"What grade did I write?" I asked.

"D+," he answered.

"Let's look in the grade book," I said, running my left index finger down the left edge of the $9^{1}/_{2}$-by-13-inch record. At the same time, I concentrated on the right index finger on the right page. There before us, so both could see was: *Studeman, Tom* . . . On the right was *A+*.

"I wondered," I said, "how the best student in class could complain about an *A+*."

In the grade book, the student right below him finished with a *D+*. So much for astigmatism and a two-page grade book.

👑   👑   👑

During my teaching days, the good Lord had blessed me with perfect hearing in one ear and supersensitive hearing in the other. Perhaps that led me to be intolerant of any noise in my classroom—unless I made it.

Former County Commissioner John Horsley reminded me of my now lost capability—supersensitive hearing. It seemed that he and a classmate were seated opposite of one another in adjoining rows of seats. I was writing on the chalkboard with my back to the entire class. John's cohort was relating an off-color story to John. He swears I said, "That's enough, Jeremiah!"

"What did I do?" asked the culprit.

"You were talking to Johnny."

"What did I say?"

"You said . . ."

John alleges I repeated Jeremiah's last sentence *verbatim*.

Oh, dear, thought I; both of those kids are sons of faculty members. If they tell about this in their homes, their parents will be sure to think I know the story. In this religious Fundamentalist area that objects to the PE teacher using her class hours to teach girls dancing, I could be fired.

🦢   🦢   🦢

"Please open the window, Lila," I said one warm day after lunch.

Lee Dormaier, Lila's younger brother, without hesitation got up, walked over to the window, and opened it. On his way back to his seat the whole class giggled. One curious student queried Lee before I could thank him.

"How come you opened the window? She didn't call your name."

"Oh, I knew Miz Southworth meant me. She always calls us by the name of the brother or sister she had the year before."

He was right. He was the third Dormaier I had had. That incident didn't stop me. I wonder how many times I called Bootsy, Lee—or how many times I called Bob, Bootsy.

In the spring when Bob was running for student body president, one of the speakers for his nomination was absent from school the day of the nomination assembly. Consequently my son, Dick, who was conducting the meeting, left the microphone in the gym to come and ask me to speak for Bob.

"You want him to win, don't you?" I asked Dick.

"Sure, he's my choice and this year's student council's choice for next year's 'prez'."

"Then, no."

"Why, Mom? I know you like him."

"Because I'm faculty. Student council represents the students—not the teachers."

Bob won. He took the gavel from Dick at the next assembly for the student body, signifying Bob would be the president of Central High's student body next year.

About ten or fifteen years later, Bob reappeared as Mr. Robert Dormaier, principal of the Christian school halfway between our home and Central High. He invited me to speak to his teenage prayer breakfast. Then I was to take a station-wagon load of upper-division students with me to Central.

Wednesday morning arrived. I could not remember whether Bob said it started at 7:00 or 7:30. His church was adjacent to the Christian school, where the event was to be. An early riser anyway, I decided to arrive a little before seven.

There was not a car in sight when the station wagon halted between what I thought to be the front and back entrances. The only light came from what I supposed was a kitchen window. A good speaker was on a Christian radio station. I turned off the engine and lights and settled in to listen. Soon a car drove in practically to my rear bumper before stopping.

Its driver rapped on my left window. I rolled it down.

"Is this your car?" he asked.

I nodded.

"May I see your driver's license?"

"Surely," I said, fumbling in my big purse.

"What brings you here at this early hour?"

It was pitch black out—just before daylight savings time switched to standard for the winter.

"A teenage prayer breakfast," I said, still fumbling.

"Teenage prayer breakfast!" he roared the first word, then softened until the last syllable was a mere whisper.

Simultaneously his powerful flashlight blinded me. He must have been scanning the more-salt-than-pepper bun of hair at the nape of my neck while I searched. I found the license and handed it to him. He mumbled my address from the license and asked me if I knew Lincoln Samuel Madison.

"I don't believe I do," was my reply.

"That's funny," he exclaimed. "He lives just a few houses from your address."

His tone gave him away; he didn't believe a word I had said.

"What does he look like?" I wanted to know.

He began to describe a thin grandchild of one of my neighbors. The young man was always having auto accidents. Hence, the patrolman knew him and where he lived.

"Oh," I said. "I didn't know his name was Lincoln. We've always known him as Skinny Sam."

Just then Principal Dormaier drove up, followed by several cars. My former student, now grayer than I, verified my story.

Bless the patrolman. He told us that he had responded to a complaint about a peeping Tom on the next road over from ours. He had seen my car lights go on and leave slowly over our bumpy quarter-of-a-mile drive. Hence, he had followed me at a distance. My mistake about the time of the breakfast caused the patrolman to mistake me for a peeping Tom.

❧   ❧   ❧

My mistakes in teaching didn't end when I "graduated" with the class of '78 from Central High. A few years later, staff members in the district called me back to tutor English to foreign-born students in the two senior highs. A Dormaier came to my rescue again. This time it was Earl, the oldest of the Dormaiers, who always tried to please me.

(Reader, you can read more later about my favorite teaching—the foreign-born students.)

I had spent from 7:00 A.M. to 8:00 A.M. at Central. Arriving about ten minutes later at the new high school, I could not find my big three-hole notebook. It functioned for lesson plans and lesson records. Without it, I was at a loss to tell who was where in which text.

Immediately I called Central's librarian. A social studies teacher whose class was doing research there answered the phone. He searched the study cubicle I had occupied before school. He also accompanied several of his students down flights of steps, searched the parking lot, and even inspected the short hill to the main road. He must have known that often I put books atop the Jeep Wagoneer while I struggled with the key on the driver's door.

A few minutes after he hung up the phone, bus driver Earl Dormaier slid his tall body through the bottom half of the Dutch door into the library conference room where I tutored foreign students.

"Is this your notebook?" Earl asked from his full height. He handed me my prize notebook just in time for my second student.

"Where did you find it?" I asked with astonishment.

"At the corner of the bottom of the hill on Hill Road, where you turn to go on the road this school faces. I figured some kid lost it, so I stopped the bus. You're the only Jen Southworth I know. I knew you were teaching foreign kids here."

We both marveled at the great God we have. Nothing was missing, no tire marks on the notebook—only a small corner of the cover was smirched with mud. Let the record show I thanked God and Earl Dormaier for their kindness. This time I had no fear of being fired. I was a volunteer tutor.

Chapter 6
Faculty

Nadine Topness Koenig recently told me this incident I'd forgotten. It must not have been too long before I "graduated" from Central High, because it happened in the hall between the big stage and the gym.

There was a mandatory assembly. As usual, the usually late Mrs. Southworth was just getting to the gym after rounding up strays who wanted to be elsewhere than in the gym. She met a tall young man dressed in a suit. He was on his way outdoors. Nadine said that I blocked his path and demanded, "Why aren't you in assembly?"

"I'm a substitute, and I didn't think it necessary," he said.

To which I replied, "Now I've heard everything in the excuse line. That's a new one. You get in there *now*!"

Nadine laughingly said of her cousin, the substitute, "He *got*!"

Fifth period was the most disliked class of the day in beloved Central High School. Teachers disliked it. Students abhorred it— even if it was their favorite subject. Their stomachs, instead of their heads, were at work after lunch.

One fifth period a terrible crash followed a loud thud in the sewing room. I left my class immediately to go next door.

There I saw the sixty-year-old librarian standing atop the teacher's desk, yelling at the top of her lungs! No student paid her the least bit of attention. All eyes were glued on two large boys struggling for their lives against one another on the floor. Entwined in their legs and arms was the contents of six drawers from the overturned sewing machine.

Next thing I knew, I was between the strugglers, marching them around the corner to the office. Apparently my sharp thumbnail in the ear of each had stopped the fight and raised them to their feet. Fortunately, both the principal and vice principal were in.

They greeted the three of us with, "What's wrong?"

"You fellows tell why and what you were doing when I found you wallowing on the floor," said I, and went back to class.

I figured if the sixty-year-old librarian, who was trying to teach freshman English in the sewing room, could climb onto the teacher's desk, she could get down without my help.

Fifth period was the home-economics teacher's preparation period. The librarian opened her class in the sewing room to anyone needing an English credit. Hence, the two senior boys were in that class. I have wondered why the home-ec teacher did not come from the food lab. Maybe it was because she knew the fight was caused by a nasty remark one of the fighters had made about the other's girlfriend.

Speaking of preparation periods, the first year at Central High, I spent mine in a vacant seat in Geometry Class. Had I been as fortunate as the students to have had that math teacher, I wouldn't have had so much trouble with numbers. All that teacher did was snap his fingers and recalcitrant students paid attention.

Some years later, I drove that "old-maid math teacher" through at least a dozen shades of red in his face. How? Because both of us were trying to recall an incident in a faculty meeting that might have shed light on the problem under discussion.

I piped up and said, "Hans, you remember that year you and I were roommates in room 4."

The next morning, long before students arrived, Hans was at my desk.

"Jen, I never want to hear that dreadful word again." He paused, then said, "About our being roommates."

He snapped his fingers, put on his hat, and slammed the door to room 15.

Years later I was asked to speak at his funeral. I didn't mention the word *roommates* but I thought about it. While I searched for material to use at the math teacher's funeral, Nadean Richardson Ross gave me this about said "teacher extraordinaire": Nadean was an excellent math student. I've forgotten the exact class of higher mathematics in which the incident happened. It seems she got the right answer in class to a problem by working it out in her head. It must have irritated Mr. Math because he immediately took her to task for not writing the solution down, step by step. She responded in curt teenage style, "That's the same difference."

Despite the dismissal bell, he kept her after class to explain carefully—painfully to Nadean—the opposite meanings of the words *same* and *difference*.

❧   ❧   ❧

The year after I retired, the Southworths were invited to the first-annual chamber of commerce dinner at the country club. We thought it odd, but the invitation stated prime rib so we went. Later we learned that the main speaker, the then-governor of Alaska, requested our attendance. No, he was not a student of mine. He had graduated in the spring with the class of '47, and I did not arrive until September 1947.

Our table was the last to be served. The governor's was the first. At the beginning of his speech, he asked if Mr. Math might be present. Unfortunately, the geometry teacher was then in a nursing home, surrounded by his mathematics books so he could keep his mind alert by solving theorems. The governor said that in his senior year, he and some of the boys had jacked up the hind wheels of the school bus, which Mr. Math drove morning and night. Many of the diners roared as the speaker snapped his fingers in imitation of the unforgettable teacher, who shifted and shifted—and shifted—gears in vain, saying, "Well, well. What's the matter?"

He evidently shifted gears and "Well, welled" until someone rescued him and the bus.

"Next year," the speaker continued, "I happened to be visiting some of my friends after school. We, the same guys, jacked up Mrs. Southworth's car. All she did was roll down the window and call, "All right, boys! Come and take the jack from under the back wheel.""

Luckily for me, one of the school secretaries told me that very day what the boys had done to Mr. Math and the bus. The speaker called for me to stand. I stood. For one of the few times in my life, I couldn't say a thing. My mouth was full of a big bite of delicious prime rib.

Central High has weathered two fairly jolting earthquakes. The one doing the most damage occurred during first lunch period. I thought I was having a heart attack. Apparently, one of the girls to whom I had been talking about a change in play rehearsal thought *she* was having one, too. She put one hand on the door jamb, the other over her heart, blinked her eyes, and uttered, "Oh, oh, oh, oh," as we watched the battleship-gray linoleum wave its way down the long, second-floor hall. Her "Oh's" kept time with each wave.

I started down the north stairs from the music room to the Little Theater below. The real terra cotta slab, which served as a landing, cracked diagonally from northeast to southwest with an unforgettable sound just before I stepped down on it. I really was afraid to step, but I was going too fast to stop.

The few students in room 15 were where they should have been—huddled against the inside wall, far away from the east windows. The few people in the halls were plastered against the inside walls.

The next day we learned one of the foreign language teachers yelled to his class, "Get under your desks!" Then he rushed outside and as far away as possible from the building.

Wonder where the art teacher was during the quake? She was probably in the basement lunchroom where I should have been, instead of trying to catch cast members to tell them about the rehearsal schedule.

Mrs. Art, as many affectionately called her, was a jewel. When other faculty members asked her to make a sign, a poster, or whatever, she would give at least ten reasons why it couldn't be done. On our way out of the art room door, she'd call, "When do you want it?" Then she'd come with paper, pencil, and a yardstick to take notes on what was wanted. Her Art Club students would get right on it. But I'm sure many of the fine things that came from her department—for me, at least—were her own beautifully done designs. They were far superior to my fondest dreams.

One day after school, I went in her room to order a poster or play program cover. She couldn't locate her yardstick. Merton, a student who lingered often after school in her room, was cleaning the sink. He didn't look up until she said, "I know, Merton ate the yardstick!"

"I did *not!*" he came back defensively.

She and I turned our backs to grin at each other.

❧   ❧   ❧

There was a morning in May when Bertha Street came to school without her skirt. Bertha seemed older in those days than I feel now eighteen years after my retirement. Now I can understand her forgetfulness.

One of her girl students lured the maiden-lady to the chalkboard to write something. Miss Street was not only in plain view of her class, but of passersby in the hall through the open door.

When the giggling and snickering reached a goodly volume, the girl whispered in the teacher's ear the cause of the uproar. I don't recall who went—the teacher or the student—to the office so the teacher could hurry home to put on her skirt.

After school that day, she defended herself at the faculty meeting with, "I was adequately but improperly dressed." Indeed, she was. Both white skirts were of the same material and pattern, except the under one sported lace at the hem. The outer one did not.

Both principal and vice principal laughed at that faculty meeting. They guffawed—or started to—at a faculty meeting the last day of school another year.

Chapter 7

Irate Faculty

D ue to no fault of the advisor, Mrs. York, the yearbooks failed
to arrive the last day of school as the advisor and her student
staff had planned. All the faculty had applauded her when they
learned she had provided time for the six-hundred-plus students
to sign each other's yearbooks. No matter that 550 of them all wrote:
"Lots of luck to a swell kid. See yah next fall."

While students were exchanging the yearbooks, teachers would
have time to sign report cards with the yearly grades. That was the
year Central was a four-year high school plus the eighth grade.

The morning bulletin suggested students clean their lockers.
Homeroom teachers would inspect lockers and return all library
books found to the librarian. But what to do with the students
who had nothing to do from cleaning-locker time until busses came
at twelve noon?

Students took the initiative. Increasing chaos preceded ten-
minute intervals of pandemonium. The intervals went like clock-
work. Filled wastebaskets from clean lockers was the signal. Metal
baskets were now ready to be rolled down the upstairs to the landing. If all the paper had not been spilled, another student would

start the basket down the next section of the stairway. Both sections of stairs were filled with squealing teenagers.

Many times my bark was heard directing students to pick up "every last one of those papers!" That was especially true when the slippery papers were too deep for my spike heels to navigate up those steps.

Although we knew naught of sonic booms in those days, I heard a sound comparable to one coming from the lower building. From the landing corner windows, I saw both principals making their way through screaming eighth- and ninth-grade girls. Both men were headed for the outside door of the boys' room in the old building. I hurried to my desk in hopes of averaging some last-minute grades. (Mine were usually the last grades to reach the office.) Hurrying availed me nothing. All report cards were mailed that year.

The art and home-economics teachers had arranged a lovely luncheon to honor our sixty-five-year-old, retiring science teacher. Mrs. Art insisted on fresh flowers for the sewing room tables. There were loads of them on the property the Southworths rented. I offered to drive home for some.

The principal had a brilliant idea: I could go if I'd take the station wagon full of kids who lived on or near our home on "the Point." It was an amazingly quiet ride for thirteen junior-high kids during the five-mile trip home. But as I neared home, there were a few exceptions: A few boys said their thank-you's and decided to get off at their driveways instead of helping me pick flowers.

Several of the gang were good friends of our son, Dick. We all understood they could stay and play outdoors at our place, if I would call their parents to tell them where they were. Then I called one of the local strawberry farms for those suddenly interested in picking berries the very next day. Telephoning was making me late for the farewell luncheon. I was not happy.

Back at school, the accomplishments of the home-ec and art teachers softened me a little. The PE teacher, who had more lockers than any of us to inspect, arrived and started to protest the wasted morning. That triggered my tirade concerning the wastebaskets. Mr. Kvinsland, vice principal of the whole school and junior-high principal, interrupted me.

With a broad grin he said, "Mrs. Southworth," as only he could inflect my name. "Wouldn't you say it's the parents' fault if students misbehave?"

"I certainly would! I'd like to tell those parents a thing or two about wasted school time and dented wastebaskets," I fumed.

No one knows what Mr. Kvinsland might have retorted. The principal, starting to join the vice principal's guffaw, slapped himself on the mouth with one hand and hit Mr. Kvinsland's arm with the other.

"Oops!" they both said.

The eighth-grade homeroom teacher wiped her eyes to conceal her laughter.

The principal inquired of her, "Don't you think he should tell her himself?" She nodded agreement.

Little did I know they were talking about the president of next year's junior-high Student Body—our son.

My husband worked swing shift, so Dick and I were home alone for an early dinner. It was graduation night, and my services were required in the mortarboard and "degumming" department. I congratulated and thanked Dick for keeping his friends outside that afternoon. Instead of saying, "You're welcome," he burst out, "Three of us guys have to pay twenty-eight dollars before we get our report cards. We don't think it's fair!"

"Why?" I asked, beginning to realize the loud boom had done some damage, hence the almost silent ride home before the noon luncheon.

This is the story as I remember it: The junior-high football center was lighting firecrackers; the quarterback was throwing them out of the boys' lavatory window at the junior-high girls. The eighth-grade homeroom teacher had sent the girls outside to pick up trash. The two principals descended from their offices to see why the girls were screaming louder than the little firecrackers. Just as the two authorities came into view, the football center was lighting a big "six-incher." The football team's end, our illustrious son, thinking to end it all, said, "Here!" and threw it into, and flushed, the closest toilet.

All three got a lesson in hydraulics as the entire receptacle shattered in the explosion. There was vitreous china and water everywhere inside and outside. That wasn't bad enough, but before I could control myself to reply, Dick went on.

"I just 'amember I have to have a white shirt tonight."

"Why?" asked I in angry disbelief.

"Well, the seniors won't be able to get out of their graduating seats to play in the band, so the band director says I have to play first-chair trumpet with the Senior High Band."

He had played baseball in his only white shirt the day before. I got one of my husband's white shirts, knowing if there had been a loaded gun in that drawer, I'd have shot our son.

Finally, as soon as Dick earned enough to pay his share of the fine for blowing up the toilet, he quit picking strawberries and his report card arrived.

As is often the case, anger can be traced to lack of communication. So it was with the late-activity bus situation during baseball season—or maybe it was football season. Anyway, the late afternoon was warm enough for the principal to roll up his white shirt sleeves and stand on the landing about half way up the front steps.

The three busses were in a line ready to leave for the 5:15 P.M. run. About 5:20 P.M. I entered the school office to add my drama announcement for the next morning's bulletin. While I was reading the day's accumulation from my mailbox, the intercom rang. I answered. The coach was calling from the gym.

"Tom and Dick are leaving the gym now. They and Harry were the last in the showers. Harry's pulling on his shirt now. When all three have passed the office door, give the driver of the head bus the high sign."

The wait was not long for Tom and Dick to pass the office, and Harry came running after. I opened the window. The driver of the first bus opened his window. I motioned with my thumb as a hitchhiker would do. He held up his thumb and drove off. Tom, Dick, and Harry were scrambling on their respective busses as they started to follow the first bus.

"Who gave the go sign?" yelled Paul Linder, the principal, whom I had not seen until then.

"I did!" was my answer.

"You're wrong! Dead wrong!"

He almost spat venom as he shook his raised fist at me and dashed up two or three steps at a time to reach the entrance doors. His red face was glistening with perspiration; the fist was still shaking.

Quickly, I beat a speedy exit down the hall to room 15. Trying to keep my shoulders from heaving with silent laughter was all I could do. He looked *so* funny! This man who was always in control, so logical, understanding, and considerate was raving, "No one but me is to tell the drivers when to leave! They've been early all week. Many boys had to walk miles home several times when they've missed the late bus."

I was sure he was angry enough to fire me.

Next morning the red-faced principal of the night before entered my room with hat in hand. He had come to room 15 before going to the office. He humbly apologized.

Athletes, coaches, and parents had complained all week about kids missing the late bus. Fed up with the situation, he thought he had found a solution. He had informed the coaches and the bus drivers that he alone would tell the drivers when to leave.

I assured him no apology was needed. I understood the situation perfectly: It was lack of communication on my part. Many times cast and crew members had missed the last-activity bus because I had insisted they perfect a few lines or work on a bit of stage business before dismissal.

When that happened and it was my fault, I drove the kid(s) home. Sometimes my old station wagon didn't reach our carport until nearly 7:00 P.M. (Praise the Lord for crockpots and preset ovens.)

I still grin when I think how funny the fist-shaker looked, as he said, "I told 'em and I told 'em and I told 'em not to leave until *I* told 'em to leave."

Despite his being the only one of seven principals I have worked under to shake his fist at me, he was my favorite of all seven.

Chapter 8

Irate Students

L et me pause long enough to state that the central administration, principals, superintendents, and school board were always
most accommodating to me. For some years, I sincerely believed it
was bartering power in our son's athletic and student-body leadership. But this event happened after Dick had graduated.

The year my mother (who lived with us) was dying, the principal and counselors gave me first period for preparation. That en-
abled me to stay home with my ailing parent until her daily caregiver
arrived. No check-in time was required.

One morning, the first bell rang as I took off my coat in my
room. The second bell for first period rang as I bounded up the
main stairs en route to the library. The hallway in front of the study
hall atop the main stairs was packed with wall-to-wall students. To
the right toward the junior-high wing were both senior-high
coaches. One should have been at the study hall desk. Two or three
other male teachers were surrounded by junior-high students.

"The last bell has rung! Get to your first-period classes," I
bellowed.

Not many tried to move as I elbowed my way through the crowd
with my usual lunchroom manner, saying, "Excuse me! Excuse

me! Excuse me!"—and projecting my elbows shoulder-high with each "Excuse me!"

Arriving at the center, I saw the real beginning of a melee. The senior-high quarterback and the team's center were glaring at each other with white-knuckled fists poised.

Fools rush in where angels fear to tread. I am no angel. Wedging my five-foot-tall and 110-pound body between them, I grabbed each young man slightly above my shoulders. My left hand grabbed Dane's shirt about his chest; the right hand grabbed Elbert's belt buckle.

"What's the matter with you two? Get to your first-period class!" I said.

Elbert's clenched fists went far over his head. He looked up and said, "Oh, God, Mrs. Southworth, don't hit me!"

Needless to say, it took all of my ham acting ability to keep from laughing. The crowd, including all the male teachers, disappeared.

No doubt I caused many students to become irate, especially because of my "no gum" rule. Clementine, "Tynee" (as she preferred to be called), was now in school. She showed up in English Class with gum in her mouth. She refused to spit it in the wastebasket at the urging of some boys.

She was a cute little thing with flashing brown eyes and a coquettish little face, framed by burnished strawberry-blonde hair. All the tenth-grade boys vied for her attention, but most of the girls were green-eyed with jealousy. Knowing boys will be boys, I watched her jaws. Boys love to tease girls and teachers.

After roll call and attendance had been posted, I asked Tynee to read the first paragraph of her theme. It was then I saw the gum on her tongue. Today, I would be hauled into court for cruel and unusual punishment. Student embarrassment worked wonders.

"Tynee, please go to the wastebasket and put your gum into it."

"I don't have any gum," she replied.

Stepping up to her, I surprised her by pulling open her mouth. The gum was in plain sight.

"Get rid of that gum *now!*" I said.

Her face was redder than strawberries. Still, she sat defiantly. I helped her from her seat and insisted she remove the gum from her mouth. Instead of the wastebasket, I escorted her to the chalkboard.

"Place the gum on the board."

She slowly did.

"Now, put your nose in it."

Then I met real defiance. She met more as I pushed her cute little nose into the wad.

"Stand there until you've earned permission to return to your seat."

Tynee finally cooperated. That was the end of gum chewing (that I detected) in any of my classes for the rest of the semester. Did I catch all the gum? Probably not.

Why did I hate gum so passionately? Six back molars are missing in my mouth because I outsmarted my high-school teachers. Bad breath was with me always unless I had half a stick of doublemint or spearmint stashed between my back teeth. Never once was I caught by a teacher—only by dentists in days before sugar-free gum.

❧ ❧ ❧

Joe-Joe was angry with me twice: Once when he was a sophomore and two years later, when he was student-body treasurer. The first happened on a hot, windy September day, when he was late to class with a properly signed tardy slip. With great gusto, he opened the door. Every paper in room 4 flew at least two rows from the door, or out the open windows.

Knowing escape from the last class of the day was what he desired, I denied him the privilege when he volunteered to retrieve the outdoor papers.

I asked two dependable girls to gather the papers from the lawn and to return quickly. Over Joe-Joe's protests, they hurried out. He was still at the door enjoying the draft.

"Please close the door, Joseph. Then go out in the hall and open the door gently," said I.

He did.

"Complete the same procedure again."

After the third "again," he asked "When can I sit down? This is no fun."

"When you've completed seven more openings and closings without complaint," I replied.

As a senior he told me with great glee that my creative dramatics event had gone one-cent behind, putting the Thespian Troupe in debt.

"The Thespians can't afford to be in debt," I said, drawing a penny from my purse and laying it on the counter.

"Mrs. Southworth! You have no idea how many entries I have to make in the books for one lousy cent," he almost wailed. (Joe-Joe was good in dramatics, having played the lead in the junior-class play the year before.)

The next morning there was a curt note in my box: "All entries made. Thespians no longer in debt."

👑   👑   👑

Debate was great the last eight years of my Central career. From 1970 on, we managed to earn our way into National Forensic League in debates, and financially to the State Tournament Yearly. For quite a few years before that, Central was the low team in our league—mainly because it was completely an outside activity. I agreed to sponsor debate if it could be a daily class. Otherwise, it would have been dropped from the school.

Maggie was known as a good kid to all Central High faculty members who had had her in their classes. Although she always did her best, she never made the top ten. She had a good clear voice and a friendly smile. I was glad to have her in both my drama and debate classes. She earned membership in the National Thespian Society.

Because her boyfriend had been a debater the year before my sponsorship, Maggie had enrolled: He graduated during the first year of my coaching. Maggie enrolled again. Two of her boyfriend's friends also enrolled. Both were certain they knew more about debate than the new debate class texts or I. If that be true, they hadn't learned etiquette. Neither had Maggie.

One class period Maggie and Jane were in a practice debate against Irvin and Max. The boys were doing everything to distract Jane. A few sharp words from me made the boys desist until Maggie arose in rebuttal. The boys whispered about Maggie just loudly enough for her—not me—to hear. Finally Maggie took a deep breath, looked straight ahead at the chalkboard, and loudly said: "Will my *unworthy* opponents please *shut up!*"

❦ ❦ ❦

The Southworths had just arrived in the Central School District when Mr. and Mrs. Jack Rhodes adopted a baby boy. They named him Webster. Recently, he told me this incident:

He was entering the high-school building when he encountered me.

"For what are you looking, Webb?" I had asked.

"For your English classroom," he answered.

"For heaven's sake, Webb! I used to hold you on my lap. Now I have to look *up* to you!"

He said that he had looked up and down both halls and thanked heaven that there was no one else in sight.

"Fourteen-year-olds are so easily embarrassed, ya' know," he said recently. "I would have died if I thought anyone else heard you. Now, it's a precious memory."

Chapter 9

Confessions

Recently at a huge memorial service for one of my lovely former student girls, three of her schoolmates had confessions they had kept from me since the 1950s. One of them I suspected, and the last one I had managed to forget.

The two Marsh sisters, Mary Lynn and Sarah, had done similar things. Mary Lynn confessed the first. She said I had called her to read her story. She must have taken a paper to the lectern with her to read, but talked the story instead. When she finished, she alleges I told her I wanted a copy of her story because what she had "read" was so good. She had to wrack her brain to remember what she had said.

Then Sarah spoke, "I did the same thing."

Because the younger Marsh was an excellent ad-libber, I think I said or did nothing. She stuck to the Drama Department through thick and thin for the three years she was at Central High. No matter what her assignment on stage, back stage, or off stage, Sarah did her best as a thespian.

Reintroducing Earl Dormaier and his wife to Walt that same night, I said, "This is the kid whose arm I had to twist to play a part in *Night of January Sixteenth*."

I had remembered talking to Earl and Irvin Winters, whom I had also wanted to try out for that play. Both boys were at a home football game when I stated, "Earl's going to try out, aren't you?"

"I don't know if I will or not," he answered.

Both he and Irvin took well-deserved curtain calls at each performance of *Night of January Sixteenth*.

The same night the Marsh sisters confessed, Earl told me loudly, "The only reason I was in that play was because you said, 'You want to graduate, don't you?'"

I *should* have been fired for threatening a student like that.

☙ ☙ ☙

Last Sunday after church, Ken Wilkinson, whom I hadn't seen to talk to for years, greeted me with: "Is it up to one hundred by now?"

Immediately, I knew the event. It was pushups. One day after lunch, a young lady in English Literature Class asked, "Is it true that you do pushups every day?"

"Yes," I replied. "Since I am middle-aged, I have to do them daily so I can demonstrate and critique my drama class when they study exercise."

"Aw c'mon. I bet you can't do any. . . . If you can, show us."

I did *five* right then and there in front of the class. Since I am not a betting woman, no money or favors exchanged hands. To this day I don't know if it was Ken who bet me or another male student.

Maybe it was Ken who, five or ten years later, asked if I had done *fifteen* in lit class. The myth grew. As the years increased so did the number of pushups. But no one ever challenged me in Literature Class again. However, as long as I taught drama, I had to demonstrate.

☙ ☙ ☙

Recently, at a forty-five-year class reunion, both a former student and former coach reminded me of this incident. It probably happened at the end of track season in 1950. Jerry Studeman never handed in a book report that I had demanded. I had told him he couldn't go to a track meet unless he turned in a book report. The night of the reunion he said, "I never did hand in that book report, but I went anyway."

"How did that happen?" I wanted to know.

Coach Beamer, standing behind Jerry, said, "Jerry went to see you; I went to see you; the principal went to see you."

"You were adamant," Jerry broke in, "so we went to the office. Then another English teacher went to see you. The office transferred me to the other English teacher's class. So, I went without the book report."

"Did you win your event?" asked I.

"Yes! I broke the record. That record stood for a long time, but I'm sure it's been broken since."

"Congratulations!" my husband and I said simultaneously.

"No wonder Bink (Mr. Beamer) wanted you to go, Jerry. That gave him a day away from school, too," I added as Beamer and Studeman beamed, shook hands, and congratulated each other anew.

Discussing the track meet incident, my sports-loving husband reminded me of another young man who almost missed his Senior Sneak five years later. Why our son Dick thought he was more privileged than other students in my senior English class, I'll never know.

His requirement was to turn in his term paper before traveling to British Columbia. He did. But he had to stay up all night to do so. No wonder he protested so loudly that Walt confirmed what I had said. We learned later that Dick slept all the way on the ferry from Seattle.

"Guess I was an adamant teacher," I admitted to Walt.

"No, you were a teacher who stood by your principles," he grinned.

His answer really surprised me. I was sure he would say, "That shows you're stubborn."

Principles, my foot! Let the world know this is my confession—now that it is too late for Central School District to fire me for evil intent.

It happened in class—room 19—sometime in the late '60s or '70s. If it had been connected with drama, it would have been a belly-laughing, slapstick farce. That year there were nineteen teenagers forcing me to make nine different lesson plans for the same first period of the morning. All needed a sophomore, junior, or senior credit in some part of English basics.

Wonder of wonders: It was the first time eighteen of them were doing the thing that they had been assigned. Only Orville was doing his own thing. I had just talked quietly and encouragingly to him to get busy. He just *had* to sharpen his pencil. It took between five and ten minutes to achieve the ultimate point.

Days before, he had been isolated in the middle of the three rows of desks perpendicular to my desk. En route from the sharpener to his desk, he placed a hand on each pair of desks across the aisle from one another. His muscular shoulders propelled him forward to the next two desks as he lifted both legs out in front of him. The good Lord knew my patience with that kid was exhausted. The Lord's patience must have been exhausted with me, too.

Forgetting that the custodian had just waxed the floors and that I was wearing a tight skirt, I quickly tried to plant my right foot to the seat of Orville's pants. Both feet went out from under me! I landed on my back and slid under his outstretched legs. Looking up at his astonished face, I put my finger to my mouth in the sign of silence. Miraculously only Orville saw my big downfall.

Quickly he helped me up and asked quietly if I had been hurt. I have since wondered if he knew that I fell trying to kick him. Had Orville not been a product of a fine Christian home, I could have—and probably should have—been fired.

👑　👑　👑

English teachers galore raised their hands in horror. They shook their heads negatively whenever or wherever I mentioned a "creative term paper." If they had dared, they would have imitated teenagers and said, "There ain't no such animal."

All my college-bound seniors would have told them the assignment: It was to choose an incident in their own lives, transfer it to another character different from themselves, place it in a different period of time, and in a different country. The latter two requirements made library research necessary. It was a review of the processes learned the previous semester, such as note taking and paraphrasing, besides footnoting. (That was in the days when footnotes were at the bottom of the page.) Of course, quotation marks and complete indentation for copied paragraphs were required.

A few finished products I recall with delight. One character was a tulip. Its authoress worked after school and on Saturdays in a greenhouse. She wrote of the tulip's adventures of being snipped in Holland, packed and transported to London, and used as a decoration in the cathedral for Queen Elizabeth II's coronation. She searched old newspapers, *Life* magazines, *World Book,* and *Encyclopedia Britannica.*

Another student had had a misfortune on a trip. He also had a missionary uncle who had a three-legged camel. He imitated the style of writing in the King James Version of the Bible. He described Sam-u-el, his three-legged cam-u-el (from a limerick we had in class) in the land of the Hueyikus in the country of Linderio. Of course, everyone in class recognized the faculty twisted names. For the life of me I can't recall what he did with my name; the time was during my reign.

Recently John C. Wierman, head of the Mathematical Science Department at Johns Hopkins University, called me when he was visiting his family. I quizzed him about his many travels in foreign countries. He had read and spoken about math in Japan, China, Sweden, Germany, Poland, Belgium, and the Netherlands, besides the International Academy of Science when it met in Oxford, England.

In our conversation he told me that in 1967 he just could *not* find six sources for his epic poem *A la Chaucer.* His solution? It was not scientific—but creative. He made up two sources!

❧   ❧   ❧

Skip Lampman phoned me the other day to verify something he thought I had said in class. With me it was not original. It was from Shakespeare's *Hamlet*. The section in act 1, scene 3, where Polonius gives advice to his son, Laertes:

> This above all—to thine ownself be true;
> And it must follow, as the night the day,
> Thou canst not then be false to any man.

After he had copied the quotation and its source, we continued to reminisce. Of course, the egg-rolling incident emerged.

Skip, after graduating from Central High School, came back five years later as Mr. Lampman, shop and study hall teacher. One day he came down from study hall to ask advice. The study hall seated 110 students. Aisles between the five or six long rows of seats served as a marvelous alley in which to bowl beebees. That day, the bowling balls were raw eggs.

"Search each student," was my cryptic advice.

"I can't. Half of them are girls," he said woefully.

That young male teacher would have been fired for pawing high-school girls.

"Will you help?"

Of course I would, and did.

Mounting the steps, we agreed on a plan. He would divide them by sex: the boys with their backs to the windows along the south wall; the girls with their backs along the north wall. He declared they would be searched. We had agreed to slap each pocket on each student whether or not the pocket bulged. I don't recall if Mr. Lampman found or took any eggs from the boys. My lot was different.

After tapping pockets on skirts, sweaters, and dresses, I saw a few girls become protective of their purses. I demanded each girl to open her purse. About a third of the girls gladly cooperated as I moved from the foot to the head of the line. Then I was in front of a tall queenly girl with long dark hair covering her shoulders. Her face I could not see. She was holding her handbag by the handles so high I could not have seen into it if she had opened it. But it was not out of my reach.

Clap! My hands connected on each side of the leather handbag. Those nearest heard cracking eggshells. Rumor has it that there were half a dozen eggs in it. Only the tall girl knew how many. That was the end of the egg rolling.

❧ ❧ ❧

Colleen Langill Mey confessed that in one of the student-body elections, she was nomination chairman for "Roe for Vice President." She failed to state how she got into drama storage (i.e., using my key, the football coach's key, or by one from the custodian).

Borrowing costumes without permission was not Colleen's style. Maybe she did not have enough money with her for the costumes she needed for the nomination skit. (The usual charge was one dollar for one complete costume. If the costume was returned in good condition, the dollar was refunded.)

Because I try to forget unpleasant situations, especially for first-time offenses, I don't remember any of this incident. Colleen assured me that after her encounter with me, she never again took anything without permission. Wonder what I did or said to her? She, her daughter, and granddaughters still patronize live theater.

Chapter 10

Incidents

One year Central High School was the location of a true Hansel and Gretel mystery. It occurred only at lunchtime. Each day a fine, white, powdery substance appeared at the right side (about six inches from the wall) of the stairs. It extended all the way from the bottom step by the cafeteria, up through the landing, and sometimes up to the second-story hall. It resembled chalk dust. Custodians hated it.

For some reason, I started back to my room earlier than usual from lunch. I ended up later than usual. As I hurried, I clearly saw the source but didn't recognize the substance. The white powder was dropping from the right powerful hand of the older Bronski boy.

He and his "little bud" were known as Big Brawn and Little Brawn because both Bronskis were so strong. All of their classmates and some of their teachers—especially the football coaches—delighted in calling them Big and Little Brawn. Big Brawn was admired on the gridiron for his giant size, strength, and grit.

Fascinated by the grinding motion of that giant hand, I followed that hand up to the second floor. Then Big Bronski transferred another handful of soda crackers from his left to his right hand, preparing to make more powder. (Those hands later transferred pigskins professionally.) He, crackers, and I hit the top step of the second floor simultaneously.

"Stop making that mess!" I commanded.

He was off like a shot on the top-floor hall of the west wing. My two-and-a-half-inch, snakeskin pumps were in hot pursuit. He started down the west stairwell. Fortunately for me, his descent made it possible for me to reach his shirt collar from behind. He stopped. Then he listened to my tirade as we returned to the upper hall custodian room. I told him that he would have to clean each step with a broom and dustpan.

As I picked up the tools, I realized he hadn't entered the custodian's quarters. Outside in the hall, I heard him through the open door of the adjacent boys' room.

"Man, that little woman should turn out for the Olympics. She ran me down in her spike heels!"

Undaunted, I tore into the boys' room, reached above my shoulders, grabbed his belt in the middle of his back, and tugged him out into the hall. (A woman teacher in the boys' room—I could have been fired!)

He began cleaning the powdered crackers as the bell rang.

Another noontime adventure comes to mind regarding another year and another star athlete—a wrestler.

It must have been the first snowfall of the season. Snowballing was allowed only on the football field or on the tennis court. There was quite a commotion at the corner where the east hall met the main hall—six to ten feet from the east entrance. The first bell rang, ending first lunch period.

Just as I emerged from room 15, a wet snowball swooshed by, barely missing my nose.

"Who threw that snowball?" I yelled.

Actually the volume could have been saved. All was deathly silent. Getting no answer from the dozen or so boys, I commanded, "All of you get into my room—on the double!"

No one had to be told to sit down. They sat. All maintained their silence. I uttered the same question again and again to no avail. Students arriving for my fourth-period class didn't enter. They merely assembled outside the door.

"You'll sit here until the Fourth of July unless the guilty party confesses."

Rusty's face was almost on his desk as his trembling hand appeared slightly above his very red ear.

"All right. The rest of you may go, but tell my fourth-period students to remain in the hall until I open the door."

Left alone, I continued.

"Rusty, didn't you hear this morning's bulletin regarding snowballs?"

He nodded affirmatively.

"Don't you ever, ever do that again! Now, get out of here!"

The last bell rang. He obeyed with haste.

Fifteen or so years later, my husband and I traveled to the district wrestling meet. Whom should I see in the hall heading for the gym in the high school but Rusty. Both of us recognized the outstanding wrestling coach in his own school. Neither of us could think of his name.

Not wanting to embarrass him in front of his male companion by calling his nickname, I reached up behind him and tapped him on his left shoulder saying, "If you're who I think you are, 'Hello'!"

He jumped at the sound of my voice. Instantly he twirled and faced me.

"Oh, no! Mrs. Southworth, I'm still scared of you."

Thereupon he proceeded to tell my husband and the other man the snowball story. Only he had more to his version:

Rusty had left my room on the run, only to be hailed into the principal's office.

"And you, student-body president, should be setting a good example to the other students. Why were you running?"

When the principal learned, he covered his mouth with his hand and wrote a special *not*-tardy slip for Rusty's fourth-period class.

I still don't know to this day if Rusty was the real culprit, or if he took the blame so they could all leave and get to class on time.

◆   ◆   ◆

Recently when Dr. Larry Gorman was asked if he were willing to be written about in this book, he said, "Sure, and include this one, too."

His inclusion is recorded first, and he claims that the incident happened near the end of a lunch period, adjacent to room 15. (That would make it the same spot as the snowball event.)

He and some other fellow were fighting. They were encircled by onlookers and probably eggers-on. The commotion caused me to open my classroom door and try to restore order in the hall.

Larry swung back to deliver his fist to his opponent's face. The "face" either felt my presence or ducked. Larry swears his fist grazed my left breast. Certainly had he connected, I would have remembered! Anyway, he turned, fell to his knees first, and then crawled on his stomach between many feet and legs to the office door.

The incident I asked permission to tell had occurred following the final performance of a play. Larry had played either the lead or the secondary lead in it.

For years my policy was to take home all cast and crew members needing a ride. Another part of the policy required cast and crew to strike the set and put away all props before they could leave for the cast and crew party after the final performance. (Usually the play ran for five performances.)

Larry's father was on the high seas. His mother had seen the opening show Thursday afternoon. Both she and Larry were depending on the Southworths to take him home after the cast and crew party.

Mr. Southworth, whom my teenagers knew as my best boyfriend, was down at the dumpster with the last load of trash from the set. Larry was sweeping the hall. Hearing a genuine commotion in the hall, I left the makeup kit to see what was going on.

Two high-school kids—who shall remain nameless—had come through the unlocked door. They were drunk. Larry, who knew they had no business in the play or even the school building at that hour, tried to throw them out. He had lost his two front teeth by the time I got to the melee. Seeing me, the two drunks did a remarkable vanishing act.

Not wanting to cause Larry's mother a couple hours of additional worry, we took Larry immediately to the Navy Hospital. The night shift there gave him something for pain and made an appointment for the next day for genuine repair. Then we took him home.

Many years later when Dr. Larry Gorman, now an osteopathic surgeon, performed a knee replacement on my husband's left knee, he told Walt that we had featured in Larry's choice of profession—through the loss of his two front teeth.

He was so fascinated the next day, with the X-rays of his teeth and bones—particularly the latter—he decided right then and there that he wanted to know more about bones. It was natural because he was pulling A+'s in biology.

At the conclusion of Walt's first knee replacement surgery, the hospital receptionist called, "Will the family of Walton Southworth please come to the phone?"

I went. She continued in a sweet, professional manner, "Dr. Gorman will speak to you now," as she handed me the phone.

Her chin dropped to her chest as her swivel chair rolled back at least three feet when she heard me say' "Hello, you Old Sawbones!"

She couldn't hear his reply: "Sawbones is right! That man has solid ebony instead of bone. I wore out a saw blade and had to send for another one. That's why it took one hour and twenty minutes longer than I thought."

He told me where and when I could see the patient. Then I hung up, returned the phone to the receptionist, and apologized for shocking her. I explained that I had known the good doctor since he was fifteen years old, and I used to kick his shins when his feet were in the aisle. Also, that he and I were, at that time, members of the same Foundation for Excellence in Education. At the monthly meetings, he usually chose to sit beside me.

After Walt's right knee replacement, he was (and still is) able to walk eighteen holes of golf, three days a week. That is no small accomplishment for a man in his eighties—especially with two knee replacements. Both of us are so glad that Larry Gorman chose to become a bone surgeon instead of a prize fighter. Walt thinks Larry would not have been too successful in the ring.

Chapter 11

Drama to Theater

Somehow the exact date has vanished. It was either during the interview or shortly after I was hired. The superintendent of Central School District had his office in the little brick building facing Hill Road. That space is now a paved parking lot. The building must have been built in the 1920s. Doubtless the stage had been constructed at the same time. It was on the west *side*—not the *end* of the gym. Immediately I took a dim view of the acoustics. From the adjacent locker and boys' room could be heard the automatic flusher. It reverberated in the gym.

Superintendent Hamilton pulled open the faded, and very dusty, red velvet curtain. Its bottom edge was about four feet above the basketball floor. The opening revealed ordinary ceiling lamps like one would expect in a bedroom. They were dim. There was no dimmer. No need for one. There were no footlights. The entire back-wall plaster was enameled. (Enamel on stage is a reflector of light, but a refractor of sound. Hence it is to be avoided.) The scene painted on the back wall was of a big, fat, pink Dutch windmill. Several smaller pink windmills dotted the otherwise pastoral landscape.

Mr. Hamilton went on about the excellent entertainment that had emanated from where we were standing. Then he asked me if I was ready to carry on? My heart sank, but I nodded a weak affirmative and said, "I'll try."

Try I did for thirty-one years, but later in the two new theaters on that campus.

Before my advent, the Class-A schools in the county did exchange assemblies. If I recall correctly, according to the athletic-league classification, an A school had enrollment between 101 and 399 students. My first year, Central was committed to entertain a slightly smaller high school on the island. Our program was put together by the Music Department and my first Drama Class.

The best actors of the latter couldn't go; they were athletes. They couldn't go, because they would miss football practice. If they missed practice, they couldn't suit up for Friday's game.

Why were they in drama class? Their body language usually, but not always, exceeded their spoken and written language. Hence their choice of drama over English or another language class. To them it was to be a snap credit for English.

The principal and bus driver insisted we wouldn't return from the island until after our school was out for the day. They were so right! But none of us four adults thought to check the tide tables against the ferry schedule. We arrived at the lowest tide of the day.

The water was so low, not a car could make it on its own power up the ramp at the island's dock. All the boys from Central, our bus driver, and the male music teacher did stevedore duty in unloading the nine cars up the ramp and onto the station dock. Try as we would, together with all the female riders' muscle power included, the fifty-passenger school bus refused to budge. At the ferryboat captain's suggestion, all Central students and two teachers climbed off the ferry and stood in the gentle rain until a bus from the host school came.

It was smaller than Central's bus, but we all squeezed on with the band instruments, including the bass drum and baby carriage— a necessary prop for the Drama Class playlet.

The instrumental and vocal groups did well; the acrobatic dancer excelled. Praise the Lord, the playlet was far better than the last rehearsal.

The day before, the music teacher had insisted we do a performance for Central's student body. All went well until the male lead in the play flubbed his lines. The female lead slapped her thigh and cackled loudly. That did it! I closed the front curtain and announced out front, "I'm sorry that I haven't trained my drama students well enough to continue the program. You students are to return directly to your sixth-period class now. . . . No, you are *not* excused to leave school until the dismissal bell rings for the busses."

Back stage I said to an amazed cast, "Look at your scripts. Read the trouble spots at least three times. Roland, read at least five times the line you blew. We'll start with Bella's line before Roland's now infamous line. We'll rehearse from there to the end—twice. If your speeches aren't word perfect by tomorrow, none of us will go to the island. Study your scripts tonight at home."

En route home from the island, the cast surrounded me. Many of them voiced, and the smiles on the faces of the others told me, how glad they were that I had been so tough on them twenty-four hours before. The play had been a big hit. Our host school's applause was thunderous.

Doubtless, the rest of Central's student body and the sixth-period teachers never forgave me. Reports from the students and the music teacher probably saved me from being fired.

Maybe the foregoing incident caused the Exchange Assembly to disappear in this county. Educational theater was meant to educate as well as entertain.

⚜　⚜　⚜

After my favorite school earned its troupe number in the National Thespian Society, Central's thespians participated in three nights of one-act plays at three separate schools. Who remembers the plays or the order of performance, let alone which school played host first, second, or third? Order is not important after fifty years. It was a fun learning experience for all three of us teachers and our casts. Best of all, students learned their two neighboring high schools were not composed of the enemies intraschool sports had inferred.

Possibly that three-night stand was the scene setter for our sister thespian troupe to the south to host an area conference. Their sponsor later became State Thespian Director. For a chemistry teacher she did wonders for aspiring actors, and she was very helpful to me.

In one of the conferences at her home school, she invited Central to do a one-act play. Halfway through the action, one of our folding flats flattened and began to fall backwards. Thanks to the quick eyes and action of Lee Dormaier, the student stage manager, he was out of his front row seat and caught it. It would have fallen on a student from another school. She was trying to rescue a light cord.

Why had we taken a folding flat? Those were all we had.

The new Little Theater was rightly named "Little." The stage was twelve feet wide at the proscenium opening and only eight feet deep. True, it had a semicircular lip—not an apron—all of three feet deep in the center front of the stage. Its floor, like the rest of the theater, was covered with heavy-duty, highly polished linoleum. I would have been fired had I brought up from the old gym stage the old eight-foot canvas flats and *nailed* them to the floor!

Those eight-foot canvas monsters were ripped and emblazoned on the back with greasepaint autographs of cast and crew for decades. Although I didn't appreciate the situation then, it turned out to be several blessings.

First, they covered the enameled back wall, so it didn't have to be painted with flat stage paint for each show.

The wood shop built the new flats in six-by-three-foot sections and fastened them with double-acting hinges. The teacher and his carpenters became very interested in helping the drama and art students cover the frames with heavy muslin and then paint and stencil them. That cooperation caused a friendly bond between three departments. The Drama Department even profited financially after all the cost of materials was paid. Some of the shop boys had never seen a play. They came to performances with their girlfriends and were amazed how good the entertainment was—even though none of the flats fell over as they had anticipated.

Another blessing was students from the other two departments being enforcers of the rule: *No* autographs on the back of flats.

Often the back was a different color from the front. A change of scene was quickly accomplished by turning the flats, whether they be two-, three-, or fourfold flats.

Some parents were at first shocked, then fascinated to see their offspring deftly change scenes without a front curtain. A front curtain would have shrunk the postage stamp-sized stage by at least a foot of acting space.

As interest in drama grew, the stage was too minute to serve casts of twenty to thirty-five actors. After taking at least fifty of my drama kids to a University theater-in-the-round, I decided to seat our audience on bleachers, on the stage, and on three sides of the Little Theater.

We used the front and back doors of the theater as entrances and exits. To our delight, instead of crowding eighty-five people in folding chairs flat on the floor with poor sightlines, the theater could accommodate 125 people comfortably, with uninterrupted vision of the action. The wood shop built us bleachers in storable sections.

Praise the Lord, we could still use the ticket booth in the hall near the outside entrance—if our Friday and Saturday night shows didn't conflict with home basketball games. Later, we encountered wrestling match conflicts on Saturdays.

I remember my activities in and near the Little Theater to be both "sock-o" and "stink-o."

One Friday night my husband was sent by his newspaper to photograph a home basketball game. That gave me an opportunity to clean the cloakroom under the stairs. The Drama Department used it for paint and stage tool storage. It was immediately opposite the ticket booth and between the hall entrance and exit of the Little Theater. About five quarts of leftover glue mixed with calcimine had to be removed from a ten-quart galvanized pail.

The only way to dislodge leftover glue is to heat it. As the winter night was bitter cold, I plugged in a one-burner electric hotplate and hoped the often opened entrance door would cool the stench— at least before it wafted its way to the gym.

No wonder the opposing team and their fans from a Catholic high school thought that Central stank! The whole end of the building was enveloped in the foul odor of near-boiling cow's hoofs and horns. The odor was so bad that one of the Catholic fathers gave up trying to explain transubstantiation to me as I tried to clean a six-inch paintbrush that had been left in the pail.

Surely if an administrator or school-board member had been to the game that night, they entered and exited by the office. Otherwise, I might have been fired.

👑   👑   👑

My English classroom, old room 13 (later dubbed room 15) was the receptacle for unfinished costumes and hand props prior to plays. Unbeknown to me, they served as advertising. Not only did the curious come to plays because of what they had seen, but sometimes students also came to tryouts after school because of the interesting props.

I must confess that I consciously stirred interest in tryouts by distributing copies of the script to each of my English and Drama Classes before tryouts. My early experience of reading alternating lines with my father as he read Shakespeare caused me to conduct tryouts in much the same manner.

That procedure had three advantages over reading a part for a certain character, as in most tryouts. First, it eliminated much of the stress for the student whose heart was set on getting the part in the cast that the student had read in tryout. Second, it told me which students could understand and interpret the lines they read. (It was Earl Dormaier's saying in class: "I'd cut his throat with a dull saw" that made me so anxious to cast him in the *Night of January Sixteenth*.) Third and last, it always increased attendance at the play and, hence, revenue. Tryouts or class readings never finished the plot. Students, parents, and friends came to see the resolution. Ticket sales were real important, especially after classes earned their money by other means than class plays. Then the Drama Department grew in size and, more importantly, quality.

❧   ❧   ❧

Central High was still committed to class plays when the basketball coach read me the riot act.

"Just because I've got five guys named Joe, I can't win games without Todd. He's the best guard I have this year. He's so improved over his sophomore year. Jen, he's gotta stick with athletics. You've got the whole junior class to pick from. Don't take Todd."

"Let's let Todd decide," I answered, and held off announcing the cast members until the coach could talk with Todd.

The day before the coach's objection, Todd had come into the theater fifteen to twenty minutes late. He chose to sit several chairs back of the reading circle of those trying out. They were signing their contracts of agreement to attend rehearsals, memorize their lines, etc. Todd asked for a contract and said, "I came to read, but you didn't ask me. Why not?"

"Because the dates of this production are in conflict with an away basketball game. Rehearsals are the same time as your turn-out in the gym," replied I.

My outstanding athletic husband had told me many times that a year's layoff was curtains for a developing athlete. It had never occurred to me that Todd came to try out.

"What made you come to read?" I asked.

"All the interesting things in front of your room last year made me decide I wanted to be in a play on stage this year. Next year, when I'm a senior, I'll go back to basketball."

The coach failed to change Todd's mind.

👑   👑   👑

After devouring *Dramatics* magazine, the National Thespian publication, Central students really got into the acts. Each year we produced two three-act plays: a Christmas program (sometimes with the Music Department and sometimes without), the one-act play contest, and the traveling Children's Theater. When royalties got beyond our budget for five performances, we didn't order plays from catalogs. We went to Shakespearean scenes for big shows, and did local authors' plays or Creative Dramatics for the traveling theater.

Probably the Shakespearean production I recall most vividly was the one composed of scenes from *Macbeth*, *Julius Caesar*, and a scene from *Taming of the Shrew*. Several times Central High produced lesser-known scenes from better-known plays of the Bard of Avon.

Before then, when anyone accused me of shrewishness, my retort would be, "I haven't bitten yet."

Petruchio and Kate from the *Shrew* changed all that.

Ann Huey's and David Gentry's idea of fighting on stage was to face each other, grab elbows, and seesaw left and right arms.

"Read your lines! . . . Think. What do the lines say?" I insisted for act 2, scene 1.

Ann was certain she could never pinch Dave's buttock on Kate's line, "If I be waspish, best beware my sting."

I pinched her so she would know how to pinch Petruchio. Still, she was reticent. Therefore I called, "Lines," to the prompter and proceeded to act with David as I wanted her to do. I must have pinched him harder than I thought. David threw me over his left shoulder on Petruchio's line, "Who knows not where a wasp doth wear his sting?" And he hit me so hard with his right hand on my *derriere* on the continuation of his speech, "In his tail!" *Slap!* I got it!

I slid off his shoulder and grabbed his left hand, sinking my teeth on the underside of his wrist.

'Now, don't really shut down, Jen, or you'll tear his skin,' I told myself.

It was hard to believe my eyes when I looked at his lower arm. Six of my upper and eight of my lower teeth had not broken the skin, but little red dots outlined each tooth, not quite breaking through the surface of the skin.

Years later he would introduce me as the teacher who bit him.

Costumes were simpler for *Caesar* than for the other two Shakespearean cuttings. Nevertheless, they caused some last-minute problems—particularly lacings for the slaves' and soldiers' sandals. The latter were made from brown leatherlike plastic and reached to the calf of the wearer's leg.

Girls, earning points toward Thespian membership, had made big, round, Roman toga shoulder pins from tub butter and margarine covers. Large safety pins were stuck on the back, rickrack on the front, then sprayed with gold paint.

After securing Calpurnia's large toga pin on her shoulder to her bra strap, I climbed on a tablet-armchair in my room to pin Caesar's toga. He was six-feet-four, at least, in height. Frankie was below us struggling with seventy-two-inch boot laces that were supposed to fit into the plastic straps to resemble the Roman soldiers' calf-high sandal.

While giving verbal directions to Frankie from my lofty perch, my hand went under Caesar's tunic at the neck opening, over his bare shoulder fore and aft, even down his right arm almost to the elbow.

"What're you looking for Mrs. Southworth?" asked the mighty Caesar.

Without a moment's hesitation or thought, I answered truth-fully,

"A bra strap."

"I didn't wear one today," he answered.

Neither he nor I smiled, but I stopped searching. Somehow I managed to pin the royal purple trim of his toga to his white tunic right shoulder. Someone handed me the gold-sprayed laurel leaves, and I crowned him. He surely looked regal.

Several nights later at the cast and crew party, characters were reliving their favorite or most horrifying spots of all five perfor-mances.

"Shall I tell?" I asked.

"If you don't, I will," said Caesar.

We both did. All laughed loudly, but he and I laughed the loud-est.

Another year Esther Shafer typed Shakespeare's lines from *Merchant of Venice*. She typed, "Oh, ———— what have we here?" in the Prince of Morocco's speech at finding a skull in the casket he chose.

"Esther, why did you leave out the four-letter word in Morocco's speech?" I asked as she delivered all neatly typed and stapled pa-pers from the office duplicating machine.

"You always substitute another word for profanity," Esther said knowingly.

"Do you know another one-syllable word that the Elizabethan audience knew? If you do, we could use it, providing it fit the rhythm of Shakespeare's iambic pentameter."

"No, I don't," she confessed.

"Neither do I. 'Hell' to most people is either a place or condi-tion, according to their belief," I answered.

The first readers of the script penciled in _h e l l_. Actually, I was looking for a young man who came from a background where the word was used often. I wanted him to say *hell* naturally. Kids who came from homes where four-letter words were forbidden either over-emphasized or lowered the volume so "hell" would not be heard.

❦ ❦ ❦

I am not easily shocked. But a young female actress did shock me in the dressing room. Women and girls from the 1960s to the 1990s will not understand my reaction. A really good student seamstress brought a finished, American Civil War-period skirt into play rehearsal.

"Jump into the next scene," I commanded. "Selma, you come with Terry and me to try on your new skirt."

To my horror, Selma laid the crinoline and lace garment on the restroom floor, the waist toward her. Then she stepped agilely into it and pulled it up as she would a pair of jeans. I was all set to help her put it on over her head. Terry was not surprised at all, but I was shocked.

❦ ❦ ❦

As I wrote earlier, I'm not easily shocked, but one of the Johnson boys was. He and several other boys were transporting the double-folding short flats from the first Little Theater up the stairs to storage. That was back in the days when the Athletic Department reluctantly allowed the Drama Department to use the balcony above the football storage.

Since the ceiling was only five feet above the balcony floor, I was the only one short enough to operate topside, providing I slightly bent my knees. Wearing three-inch heels forced deeper knee bending. Whether the boys liked to see me scramble or whether there were two boys handling one flat, I don't know. They always gave my 112-pound frame a workout. Proof: The scales stopped at 110 the next day.

When we got down to room 15 so I could dole out activity-bus tickets, I went to my coat locker to remove my suit coat. My scarf had been shoved into my pocket when I was on the balcony.

John said, "Oh, don't, Mrs. Southworth. Don't take off your coat! You don't have a shirt on!"

◆　　◆　　◆

Sometimes students warned me too late. You read before about the Drama Department's creative budget, which equaled making something out of nothing. That budget forced us to produce royalty-free entertainment.

Our biggest money saver was probably the evenings of cuttings from Shakespeare. The other quality plots produced sans royalty were Creative Dramatics. Usually the drama class traveled to elementary schools, rest homes, and daycare centers. Some productions were the final examinations for the class.

All that needs to be memorized in Creative Dramatics is the order of the main elements of the story, not specific speeches. No sets are required and very few—if any—props. As in a good story, the audience must know who the characters are (by the character's own or someone else's introduction within the action); where they are; and what, when, and why the characters are in the predicament. All of that information must be given in one or more of the actors' speeches—hence, the name Creative Dramatics. Concentration is the main thing to be learned.

In 1973, our Thespian Troupe received a beautiful, big fat plum. It was a one-act play written by a local author, Paula Craig. She had been Paula Crandall, thespian understudy of Central's troupe in the 1950s. Had she written her play *Names Will Never Hurt Me* while she was in high school, she would have been a Thespian with quite a few stars.

Former Thespians will remember membership was attained only when a student had accumulated ten points: one hundred lines or speeches on stage, one hundred hours of backstage work, or a combination of the two. Each additional ten points earned a gold star. Who knows if Paula would have exceeded Colleen Langill Mey's five stars?

Paula's *Names* made use of two entirely different casts. Each cast performed at three different places. The actors liked it. Children's audiences liked the action. I loved the moral it taught without being preachy. It was not Creative Dramatics, but it taught concentration—concentration on the right thing at the right time.

During a Traveling Theater (maybe it was *Names Will Never Hurt Me*) I was guilty of concentrating on the wrong thing. Usually, my station wagon hauled the necessary props and two or three muscled male students to handle them. The station wagon was headed south on one of the many roads on the east side of the salt water that divides Central's area. Over my right shoulder I was giving directions to the boys in the back seat. Those directions concerned placing the props at the next performance, because actors had been at a disadvantage at the one we just finished.

Then my gaze turned straight ahead over the steering wheel. I saw a westbound driver's face contorted with profanity.

"What's the matter with him?" I asked.

"You went through a stop sign," chorused my riders.

"I couldn't have. I never saw it," I said defensively.

"Well, you sure did. You looked right at it!" said one of the Mastel brothers. The big Mastel family lived on the east side, so they knew where the stop signs were.

❧   ❧   ❧

Jimmy was a well-built Native American. He had shoulders any wrestler or football player would have coveted. I don't remember his name being on any athletic list. We first met in September of his sophomore year.

All the tenth graders from his area in the school district giggled when I announced he would give his three-to-five minute speech the next day. As soon as the class quieted to plan (on paper) their speeches, I asked Jimmy to stay a few minutes after school. He did.

When my sixth-period class left, here was Jimmy. I could see he was petrified with fear.

"What did you do this summer?" I asked after he finally sat on the edge of a seat near me.

"Nothin' but work," he answered.

"Doing what?" I wanted to know.

"Purse seining," Jimmy said.

"Purse seining?" I questioned; then declared, "I've heard of purse snatching but never purse seining. Tell me about it."

He did. Never did a conference with a student pass so quickly or interestingly as his face and hands kept up with his mouth.

The next day he stood tall like a totem pole and launched into the fascinating description of purse seining. His father was one of the leaders of their tribe. He must have said something about speaking to a group, or Jimmy may have watched Indian speakers. I had told him nothing about public speaking except, "Think about what you are speaking." His *twenty-minute* explanation of how the Northwest Indians catch fish commercially was the only speech to draw applause—enthusiastic applause.

Two years later, Jimmy appeared as the clerk in a major play set in a court of law. Half the Indian reservation forced us to announce before curtain time: standing room only.

※   ※   ※

Abner was fat. He probably spent more time in the library than the study hall. Chairs could be adjusted to the big tables in the library. Study hall seats were screwed to the long wooden runners so they could be moved an aisle-width for sweeping the floors. Custodians liked them. Chubby and tubby students did not. Abner was both. Doubtless it was a struggle for him to get into or out of his assigned seat.

Miss Street was Abner's study-hall teacher. Instead of a dismissal note to the library, she wrote it to room 15, to check out a play book and stay in that room the whole period. I don't recall the name of the Rowe Peterson Play Company's high-school play. One character had to be a fat teenager. Since the seats in my room were really college tablet-armchair seats, Abner decided to spend the entire hour reading the play with my class.

Of course he got the part. What I didn't expect is what a good actor Abner really was. Besides his first typecasting, a genuine change was seen in him. His attitude, poise, and appearance changed the next two years. He not only worked into Thespians, but also won stars for good performances in different shows.

After a Drama Class trip to a university play, Abner was one of the few to write a thank-you note. The thanks were for the things high-school Thespians had done for him: new decent friends who liked school, and respect from them and teachers.

I do not remember, but I hope I showed that note to Miss Street. It was really her he should have thanked.

Chapter 12

Difficulties in Drama

"Mrs. Southworth, I can't possibly kiss Alfonso!" Gineen, the petite ingenue, whispered in my ear.

It was Monday after school during the first rehearsal of act 3. She knew Central High's actors were required to kiss, playbooks in hand, the very first rehearsal of any kissing scene. That rule avoided the usual giggles of kissing in public someone the actors hadn't even dated.

"Why not?" I demanded.

"He smells so bad; it's an effort to stand near him. Ask any of the boys who are near him the most."

I did. Each confirmed her statement. One even volunteered: "He smells like a septic tank or sewer."

"Too bad I can't give him a bath," I said. "I'd be fired."

"We can," said Pete. "Just get me and Paul out of sixth period advanced Geometry Class tomorrow. Alfonso's there, too."

"He'll need clean underwear," added Paul. "I don't think he's had a shower since sophomore PE, or changed shorts either."

We spent so much time planning the next day's strategy for sixth period, we didn't get to the kissing scene. Gineen was grateful.

Before school the next day, I personally delivered an excused-absence note for the three boys to their math teacher. She gladly cooperated. She had made an appointment to see the boys counselor regarding Alfonso's stench but hadn't seen the counselor yet.

Next I went to the school's laundress. When she learned what I wanted and why, she gladly told me to tell Peter and Paul to come to her before they entered the shower room. She assured me that quite a few unclaimed jock shorts were left in the boys' locker baskets at the end of the semesters. She had washed them all. The good ones she had folded and kept, hoping some parents would call. Rarely one did. Several good ones were available.

At the beginning of Tuesday's rehearsal, I lectured on the importance of daily cleanliness. "Each actor must be nice to be near." All were encouraged to use the Drama Department's deodorant and mouthwash if they didn't bring their own each day. Alfonso, then and there—plus thereafter—made a big showing of using the department's deodorant. All three boys had wet heads. Alfonso's dripped.

Riding home with me after play practice, Peter said, "He was encrusted. We had to use a table knife to scrape his buttocks."

Whether that was hyperbole or truth, only Alfonso, Peter, and Paul know.

Speaking of wet heads, there was the spring day in 1976 when all of us got wet during the afternoon matinee of *Bicentennial Trilogy*. The three top thespians had each directed a one-act play. The program listed in order: *Politicians*, *Witches*, and *Spies*.

It rained so hard that afternoon, the baseball coach held an indoor practice in the gym, just across the wide hall from the backstage double doors of the theater. In the middle of the second play, *Witches*, a batted ball broke the window of the fire alarm in the gym. The evacuation bell split the ears of actors and audience alike.

The actor playing a New England pastor shot up off a bench and ran out the backstage door. The bench upended, dumping

Martha in her starched Puritan apron and cap on the floor. Bewildered, she scrambled to her feet.

Fortunately, I happened to be on the west side of the auditorium, so I could open one of the emergency doors to the outside.

"Clear the theater," I barked.

There was no argument from the students or adults in the audience—or from Martha. There were complaints, however, from the wet, reassembled audience, cast, and crew after the all-clear bell. Many of them, including cast member Becky Balter Meyer, thought until this year that it was a real fire drill.

Martha complained the loudest to the actor-pastor, who had jumped up and dumped her on the floor. Henceforth, she and I made sure all other actors consider their partners and sit close together in the center of the benches, whose supports made miniature teeter-totters.

🔻 🔻 🔻

Mothers can tell whether their babies are hungry, uncomfortable, angry, or in pain by the way they cry. Teaching in five public high schools taught me to recognize teenage girls' screams.

Some children take joy in just screaming. Most teenage girls and women scream from genuine pain or fright. Two such incidents happened years apart at Central High.

In the early days, Monday first periods were extended for twenty minutes for homeroom meetings or utilitarian activities. Once a month each homeroom was expected to clean some part of the school grounds. I was manning the big wastebasket on the north end of the tennis court on the east side of the building. (That area is now a three-story annex to the main building.)

Shrieks shattered the spring sunshine. I dashed southward, where one of the boys was chasing several girls. I outran him and snatched his wastebasket from him. It contained a twelve- to fifteen-inch dead garter snake. The girls were sent back to their homeroom. Lining up the boys, I walked in front of them and picked up the very dead snake by the tail.

"Which one of you boys found this snake?"

No one answered.

"The guilty party will confess, or I'll wrap this snake around each of your necks until I get a confession."

One white-faced sophomore held up his hand as the bell rang. Whether he was really guilty or fearful, I don't know.

"Never let this happen again, or each of you will *get it!*"

They all stood until I loudly said, "Dismissed!"

The other incident occurred in back of the king-sized stage of the new theater. I don't recall if the Drama Class was rehearsing or if its members were trying to rearrange backstage storage. Bruce Aamodt doesn't concur with the details. This is what I remember:

From just in front of the projection booth, center back in the audience, I heard several girls scream—several times. The shrieks came almost in staccato time but not in unison. They continued from backstage right until I reached stage center.

Bruce's six-foot-six height emerged from stage right. He held a two-by-four (or four-by-four) about eighteen inches in length. It contained a fifty-penny spike through one end. He moved as if he were going to hit me with the sharp spiked end. He was so tall, I must have jumped to snatch it from his grasp. Then he, instead of I, felt the spike.

He claims all the girls were playing along with him. Their faces as well as their screams told me otherwise—I don't believe they were such convincing actresses. But I am convinced that had the administration known that I hit a student with the pointed end of a fifty-penny spike, I would have been fired.

Many Central students and, unfortunately, a few faculty members pronounced the word *drama* either "dray-ma" or "drammer." *Theater* was variously uttered "*tea*-a-ter" or "the-*ater*" when I came.

Every year I managed to take a busload of students to a college or university play. Occasionally, a parent or teacher accompanied us. Besides being responsible for ticket money, each student had to say *theater* and *drama* correctly. The school district paid the gas for the school bus and paid the driver. If he wished to attend the play, I paid for his ticket. My husband often accompanied us, but not this time. It was a three-day trip and proved to be a real learning experience.

Much learning for students and teachers alike was gleaned from a National Thespian Conference held at the university. Certified Thespians were not the only ones eligible. Work backstage, a walk-on, or enrollment in Drama Class filled the requirements. Sign-ups and arrangements had to be made well in advance. Everyone attending was billeted for two nights at a hotel a few blocks from the campus.

Word came sometime on Saturday that Samantha hadn't come in until 4:00 A.M. the second night. When confronted, Sammy denied it and told a believable story. We learned later that the story she told had happened Thursday night, our first night there, not Friday night.

At the trip's end, our district school bus arrived exactly on time in front of the hotel on Saturday night, after the last show. All the students were loaded, plus all their luggage. (I never cease to marvel at how much luggage teenagers bring to spend two nights away from home!) Yes, we were all loaded—except for Samantha.

Looking at his watch the bus driver said, "We'll have to leave *now* if we'll make the last ferry."

En route to the ferry dock, Samantha's roommate ventured, "Maybe Sammy will be at the ferry dock. She didn't sit with our group tonight but with two soldiers [from a nearby base]. Her suitcases were gone when I checked out."

We missed the last ferry. We missed Samantha, too. That meant we had to drive around Puget Sound by land. The bus had just enough gas to return to the school's bus barn via ferry. Finding a gas station that would take our school district's voucher was a real problem. If my memory is correct, the driver and I, by pooling our finances, managed to buy enough gas to get to the high school two hours late. My precious husband and some anxious parents were waiting in the parking lot.

The hardest thing I have ever had to do in my thirty-five years of teaching in public schools had to be done. It was to go into the building at 3:30 A.M. and call Samantha's mother. She was not waiting with the other parents. They were more curious why the bus was late and no one had called. Whom could I have called? Parents had already left their homes when we discovered we had missed the last ferry. At that time there was no public telephone outdoors on the school ground.

Samantha's mother was disappointed but not really surprised. I was!

"Sammy told me not to worry," she said, adding, "Mrs. Southworth will drive home all the kids who don't have a ride. That teacher or her husband always does."

After agreeing to call each other when whoever saw Samantha first, I hung up. Walt and I drove a couple students home. He was as concerned as I. Surely a teacher who would leave a student behind at one o'clock in the morning on a field trip deserved to be fired.

Monday, Samantha missed all six classes. Shortly after three in the afternoon, when classes were over and teachers were assembled for faculty meeting, I received a phone call. Samantha's mother told me, "Samantha is home." Then she added, "She brought her new soldier-husband home, too."

Chapter 13

Other Difficulties in Drama

Next to leaving Samantha and calling her mother, other difficulties were encountered. Compared to the two worst, these were minor. Some are humorous; some are not.

The lead in *Young Abe Lincoln in Illinois* (an unpublished high-school play) didn't know how to whistle. Of all the student-body males he had the height, chin, hair, and nose for a Lincoln. But the script had Abe as a whistler. For days I would get him out of class fifteen minutes early during my preparation period. We would meet for ten minutes up in the football-drama storage room before rehearsal.

His idea of what he should do with his tongue was to curl each side of it, until the opening was the size of the head of a pin, and blow. Nothing came of the effort. Telling him to put the tip of his tongue inside his lower teeth didn't work for him either. Light dawned: I asked him to put his fingers in my mouth to learn where my tongue was when I whistled; then in his own mouth. Finally, I put my fingers in his mouth and put his tongue where it should be. That must have done it—or someone else showed him. He whistled when he lifted an ax while sitting cross-legged in the center of the stage.

Unsanitary? You are absolutely right! Today I would be fired for taking such liberties.

When Pete Manning taught wood shop, he usually delivered all stage props well in advance of the play opening date. Hence, it never occurred to Max that he might have difficulty getting out of a window-seat box. The whole side away from the audience was open. The padding of the window seat was securely fastened to the hinged lid. In an early scene, Max had opened the top and slipped into that box, which was at least six feet long.

Just prior to the end of act 2, Max was to have sat up, opened the window seat and said a line in the play *Fog Island*. The last performance came. Max did not come up to say his line. The light man said, "I waited an eternity. No Max, so I shut off the stage lights and counted from 1001 to 1050 before turning on the house-lights in the Little Theater."

He was interrupted by a member of the stage crew excitedly saying, "Come, Mrs. Southworth! Max has passed out and is just lying in the window seat. If you'll help, we can get him out of the back of the box."

Thespians sold chess pie and coffee in the hall during inter-mission between acts 2 and 3. The theater was practically empty. From backstage the stagehand and I pulled Max out the open side, away from the audience.

My helper was sent to the home-ec room for a big glass of ice cold water and cup of hot, black coffee. Max came to without hav-ing the cold water poured on his face. He wasn't in the least inter-ested in the coffee. He wanted fresh air. With difficulty—and alone—I put his six-foot, 120-pound frame up the stairs and onto the football field. The cold night air made him tremble. He in-sisted a cigarette would calm him.

Cigarettes have always been ugly in my estimation and nos-trils. But here I was trying to hold Max vertical with one hand. The other searched his pockets for his pack of cigs and his matches. He got a cigarette in his mouth but had the shakes so bad he couldn't light it. Finally, I managed to light the wooden match with my thumbnail. (Twenty years earlier I had seen our hired man do that on the farm.)

I warned him, "You could be expelled for smoking on the school grounds. I could be fired for this."

After three or four drags, he stamped out the cigarette, and I threw it someplace. Max declared he was ready to crawl into the box again from backstage—if the light man didn't turn on the backstage hot window lights until he could sit up, raise the cushioned lid, say his line, and get out and sit on the window seat. His line was crucial to the plot. The only difference was the climax came at the beginning of act 3 instead of the final line of act 2.

Years later one of Max's in-laws told me Max had doubtless been drinking. What the liquor was I have no idea, because I couldn't smell it. The whole melee was not only difficult physically but also psychologically—and before teenagers were into drugs. The show must go on, even in educational theater.

❧   ❧   ❧

The third difficulty was physical, and it led to my resignation. Sometime during the school year of 1977–1978 my husband tried to convince me I should retire. It was furthest from my desire. I love teenagers. His argument was that he planned to retire in 1979, and that I should retire first.

"Why?" I asked.

"If I retire first," Walt said, "I'd just get things the way I want them around our place. Then you'd retire and you'd change them."

"Wouldn't you do the same thing to me should I retire first?"

"But that's different," he answered. "You're flexible."

His answer didn't influence me; the following incident did.

James M. Barrie's novel, written in the 1800s, had been made into a three-act play. *The Little Minister* was just the historical drama for Central's thespians. Many of them were in advanced

Play Production Class. They studied dialects. Most of them did well with the Scottish brogue.

But several senior girls were two big disappointments. The first one was that ten of them didn't turn out for tryouts. Each one was employed after school. Their jobs conflicted with scheduled play practice. Most of the girls willingly took home material, measurements, thread, and patterns to make male or female costumes for the actors in the play.

Four performances of *The Little Minister* were scheduled starting Thursday at 3:00. (The Drama Department could not afford an extra royalty for a Thursday night performance.)

The second disappointment came the Monday of the opening week. The first of the ten girls turned in her cutout costume, claiming she didn't have time to finish it by Thursday, let alone Monday night's dress rehearsal. The nine other costumes found their way to my desk by Tuesday. Not one of those had even been cut out.

At home my shears and portable machine stopped for only two hours while I slept Tuesday night. Both tools went to school with me Wednesday. I wrote more questions on the chalkboard for each class than I knew any student could answer in fifty-five minutes. All papers were due at the end of each class period.

"Finished or not, turn in your paper," were my few words to each of the six periods.

That procedure gave me nearly forty minutes of each period to sew. Some girls in my classes basted or used one of the department's two sewing machines when they learned the situation. I had to stop for play practice for two hours after school—it was the last rehearsal. Shears and portable went home with me again. The tools snipped or hummed all night after a quick TV dinner. The only stops were my swallows of black coffee.

At 5:00 Thursday morning, I knew I had to stop to get to school at my usual arrival time. I thought a cold shower and more hot coffee could get me there. I was so tired that my left foot couldn't step over the shower curtain guard. It was four inches high. The right foot failed, too.

"Southworth, you old fool," said I aloud. "Pick up your feet and get in there!" I grabbed the sides of the metal shower stall so my arms could help me in.

"Please, God, should I resign?" I asked, turning the water on full blast.

"Yesss!" whizzed the showerhead.

Before leaving our house, I fell on my knees in the sewing room and prayed, "Dear Lord, You and I both know I bit off a bigger chunk than I can chew. But whatever happens today—opening day—I'll praise your name. Amen."

Before I arose the thought came: *Babby, my leading lady in the play, is in my first two periods this morning. I'll get her excused from music. The Music Department has had her excused from my classes a couple times for concerts. She does all right on costumes, too. . . .*

Babby didn't answer roll in either class.

Ten minutes into second period there was a knock. I left the chalkboard assignment writing to open the door. There was Babby and a woman I didn't know. My leading lady introduced me to her mother who told me, "I have today off work. I understand the Drama Department has a cabinet-model Singer just like my sewing machine at home. Can you use me today?"

"You two are an answer to an unasked prayer," said I, hugging them both simultaneously.

I knew Babby could handle the Drama Department's Viking portable machine. She had proved that for an hour the day before. I manned my own Viking portable.

At 11:00, a knock drew me from the chalkboard again to the door. The woman in the hall was a total stranger.

"My little daughter from the elementary school who plays the child in the *Little Minister* tells me she doesn't have a costume and the first show is today. I can sew a straight seam on a sewing machine. Please show me what I can do to help."

"Welcome, you angel from heaven," was my response.

We three sewed continuously. No lunch. Someone made instant coffee several times in my hot cup in the prop room. We sewed and sipped on. The stage manager set the stage when he arrived. The rest of fourth-, fifth-, and sixth-period students who weren't in the play reported directly to the library. The librarian was expecting them by name from my roll book.

All costumes for act 1 were ready when the curtain opened on time. During the first two acts and even at the beginning of act 3, all three sewing machines kept humming. All characters were properly costumed for their first entrances! My sewing angels were able to step into the back of the theater for the last half of act 3. I thanked them and glorified God for sending them.

"Thanks, too, Lord, for keeping me from falling on my face both literally and figuratively!" I said aloud as I closed the machine.

After the theater and my classroom were emptied and the last student scrambled into the activity bus, I took time to set a few things to rights on the stage. Then I worked costume racks. Both men's and women's racks revealed that several costumes needed hemming, pressing, and buttons. Said costumes, my bulging briefcase (containing four days of paper from six classes), and the portable sewing machine were put into my Jeep. My husband met me for dinner at a restaurant.

Friday there were two performances. One started at 3:00 and the other at 8:00. Although I managed to sleep four or five hours both Thursday and Friday nights, my body reacted the two following mornings the same as Thursday—trying to get into the shower at 5:00 A.M. Saturday morning I *had* to get up early. Why? Our house, after a week's neglect, was a mess, especially where the sewing machine and ironing board were. The cast and crew for the last ten years had held their party at our house following the final show. They loved our indoor heated pool. After a swim, wall-to-wall kids filled our living room and kitchen to consume the food they brought and to watch TV until 2:00 A.M.

The night of Thespian initiation closing when I usually said Romeo's line from Shakespeare's *Romeo and Juliet*: "Good night, good night. Parting is such sweet sorrow that I shall say, Good night 'til it be morrow."

That night two weeks after the play, I said the first part, but continued with, "There'll be no tomorrow for next year. Before the ceremony tonight, I laid my resignation on the principal's desk."

Slow poke that I am, it took until July 17, 1978, to clean the "shuvit" (prop room) and take the $2,000 inventory and to clean costumes and props. My keys were exchanged for my last paycheck. It was hard to realize God and the administration had kept me at Central for thirty-one years and let me resign.

I had not been fired.

Part Three
Pleasure

Chapter 14

Volunteer

S hortly after checking out from beloved Central High School, my favorite principal recommended me to teach English and social studies on the Indian reservation. Attendees were paid the hourly minimum wage while earning their general equivalency diploma. Their GEDs, as they called it, could gain entrance to the community college just the same as a high-school diploma. Teaching there was a genuine learning experience for all—mostly me. Again, our Lord was preparing me to teach people of a different culture and values from mine.

Another retired teacher was scheduled for major surgery. She asked me to be her replacement as reader for the blind manager of the Community Action Program's Handicap Office. Manager Jan LaPrath's quick ear recognized my voice before her regular reader could introduce us. Jan had graduated valedictorian from Central High the same year our son did.

Within a few weeks an announcement arrived at the Handicap Office. It stated the dates and time of an upcoming workshop for people who wanted to teach reading, writing, and speaking English to immigrants. The United States was a haven for many Vietnamese refugees at that time.

"This sounds right up your alley," said Jan.

She was so right. Not only was I certified to teach foreign-born, but also what the newly formed Literacy Council called basic tutoring to American-born. Then followed certification to teach tutors how to teach others in basic and English as a second language. Lastly, I became a supervisor in tutor training for both. I have served as a member of the board of directors of the county's Literacy Council for eighteen years.

Literacy volunteering has been the most enjoyable teaching of my nearly sixty years of teaching. Why? At least 99 percent of them *want* to learn!

👑   👑   👑

My first student was Carry Lou. Because I attempted to teach a class in psychology at Central High for seventeen years, the literacy coordinator called me for this particular student. Carry Lou was enrolled in a parenting class in the nearby community college. The court had enrolled her. She was battling for custody of a six-year-old child. Every time the college instructor would call on her to recite in class, she had an attack of epilepsy.

The day and time for our meeting was set at the welfare office. As soon as I told her she would be able to read a complete story before she left, she started to tremble, roll her eyes, and salivate. Having had several petit- and grand-mal epileptic students out of the more than five thousand students, I knew Carry Lou's symptoms were not the real thing. I put my arm around her shoulders and said, "Carry Lou, if I thought for one minute you couldn't do it, I would not have come. Seeing your handwriting and talking with you, I know you are an intelligent woman. Let's get started to read, so you can get back your child."

She stopped trembling instantly and cooperated beautifully for two hours. When I started to put things back in my briefcase, she smiled and ran out into the hall. To the first person she saw, she told, "I just read a whole page!"

The man didn't know that it was the first page in her *entire* thirty-five-year life that she had really deciphered. He was not impressed. Her husband was. About six months later the court was impressed. Carry Lou got back her child.

❧   ❧   ❧

One of my most successful and well-liked adult students was Cordell "Corky" Sunkel. He couldn't have felt the same toward me at our first meeting as he does now. It was sometime in the 1950s at a night football game that we had our first encounter.

"Hand me that lighter and package of cigarettes," I commanded. The package contained only one cigarette. (Wonder what happened to it?)

"You can get your lighter the last day of school."

Cordell did not come. Unknown to me, he was then in junior high school. That building was up the hill about a quarter of a mile from the senior high school.

Christmas 1978, despite my having "graduated" with the class of '78 the previous spring, the Central High faculty invited Walt and me to their party in early December at one of the area's better restaurants. I knew Cordell would be there because his wife, Bonnie worked the computer in the high-school office. Walt and I sat opposite the Sunkels. What an opportunity to return his lighter I had snatched from him nearly a quarter of a century earlier. That night I learned for the first time, he had been a junior-high student. No wonder he hadn't claimed it.

The following summer Cordell phoned me to ask, "Mrs. Southworth, will you teach me to read?"

There were two very good tutors in his area. They both showed excellent teaching qualities in basic reading workshops I had conducted. He brought my debating skills to a halt by saying, "I'm an alcoholic. [That's why he had been called Corky.] Alcoholics Anonymous teaches us to face our problems. You were the reason I dropped out of school. My three brothers who had you told me 'You have to shape up or ship out if you get Southworth.' I shipped out. That's why I never got the lighter and why I want *you* to teach me."

Three mornings a week from June to the first week in February he arrived at our house at seven o'clock. We started with the names and sounds of the letters in the alphabet. He quit when the winter weather was so bad he couldn't work outdoors starting at eight o'clock. By then he was reading at sixth grade level. He could write checks for his employees instead of having to interrupt his wife, Bonnie, up at school to write them. He owned his business and had three employees at the time.

Knowing I was a Christian, he hastened to tell me he had given his life to Christ after hearing a great evangelist. At that time he was reading four books at a time: The Bible, a book beside his bed, one in the bathroom, and one in his truck.

He was a dynamic seller of the literacy program and a fundraiser for the Literacy Council. Not only was he a member of the Council's board, but also a member of the Washington State Literacy Council Board. Often he and I would speak to other organizations on behalf of literacy. *Money Magazine* did an article on Cordell Sunkel because he had increased his income from $50,000 a year to $200,000 after he learned to read.

Because of his success, Cordell's son-in-law wanted to complete his education by earning his general equivalency diploma.

The younger man had dropped out of school during the end of his sophomore year. He had already completed the literature and grammar section of the GED text when his literacy tutor suddenly died. The young man appealed to me. Like his father-in-law, he came to our house at seven o'clock on his way to work in the morning. He progressed very slowly because he loved to argue. Finally one morning I asked, "Young man, why do you get up an hour earlier three days a week to come here on your way to work?"

"To finish and get my GED," he answered.

"Then let's learn what's in the book. You can't learn unless you keep your ears, eyes, and mind open and your mouth closed," I pointedly said.

Not too long after that, he eagerly memorized the multiplication table. We both worked on that through multiples of fifteen. He told me with pride one morning that he was able to get the right answer to problems in his work before others obtained the same answer with a calculator.

His wife invited Walt and me to their home for a family celebration of his new diploma. I'm not sure, but that might have been the time I learned that through the Testing Department at the university, Cordell was told he would never learn to read. Praise the Lord I didn't know that. I treated him as I did all beginners— and he reads!

My next student was from "El SalBator." On her arrival for the second lesson, Rosa exploded with, "Why from 'keendergarten true beeznees colletch' no one 'tal' me a 'latter' have a 'soun'?"

"Who were your teachers?" I wanted to know.

"Da Seestersss," she answered.

"From which country?" was my next question. She had a lilt that I thought might imitate Irish nuns.

"The Natibs," she replied.

What a time she had, like most Spanish-speaking students, saying the sound of a final *d*. Most Spanish ESL students make the sound of *dth* for a *d*. When she came to the name David in a simple story, she said "Dobby." She knew I must be wrong because, "My coosin eez Dobby. Heez name spell same."

Apparently we say "Davey." A tape recorder helped. After who knows how many days, she telephoned me from her uncle's house and said, "Leesun: 'Davi*d*.' I don't say 'Davi*dth*' anymore."

Doubtless her North American relatives had helped her, too.

Two God-incidents are connected with Rosa, my "Salbatorin." One, her father's brother had married a woman whom I had babysat when I was a teenager; two, that same aunt was the daughter of my fourth-grade teacher back in the Midwest.

Bless my El Salvadorian's heart. Her relatives here were Protestants, but they saw that she got to Roman Catholic Mass on Sunday. Unfortunately, she could not understand the priest. When teaching literacy background at Central High, I bought a Catholic

Bible. I wanted the tenth-grade class to feel comfortable with the version of their denomination. It would be hard to find a happier person than my El Salvadorian when she learned how to compare the English with her Spanish version—book, chapter, and verse.

Rosa's mother was ill. Rosa was afraid to return to El Salvador, which was then torn by civil war. The day of her last lesson, I took both her hands in mine and prayed for her safety. Later, word came that she had had a safe drive home from the airport in another town. She arrived home on the one and only day there was no fighting over the road she traveled. That road had changed hands many times that same week. Coincidence you say?

"God-incidence," say I.

The next year, the telephone rang on my birthday. It was hard to believe Rosa was calling from El Salvador. She sounded more like she was calling from her uncle's home about four miles away. She called to "weesh happy birthday to my sweet, sweet, funny, funny, teacher."

👑　👑　👑

Not only was I a funny, funny teacher to my Salvadorian, but a genuine mystery to an intelligent Korean sophomore a few years later. Tutoring him at one of our district's high schools, I became disgusted with my inability to remember where I had put things (i.e., pens, pencils, marks in exact pages, books, etc.). My pet word for such times is *phooey*. After I had used it several times, he was really puzzled.

"What is *phooey*?" he asked.

"Oh, it is just a word I say when I'm mad at me," I answered.

"You mad at you? Why?" There was surprise in his voice.

"Because I make mistakes or can't remember where I put things," I answered.

"Teachers *never* make mistake," he said with a tone of authority.

"This one does," I replied.

"But teachers never say, 'Teacher make mistake, when teacher make mistake," he rejoined.

"This one does," I retorted, pointing to myself.

Two years later this brilliant physics student won first place in the county, then the state physics fairs. He qualified at a national competition to enter his project in the International Physics Fair shortly after school let out for the summer.

On his return from the international competition, I telephoned him to learn how he had fared. I thought I detected tears through his voice. He had placed only tenth.

"Tenth place in this modern scientific world is very good," I started to congratulate him.

"They didn't understand me," he added in muffled tones.

"Why didn't you come to me for help in speaking?" I queried.

"Because you don't understand *fractals!*"

He was right. Just now I had to call the high school to learn how to spell *fractal*. To place tenth in an international competition of any kind is no small accomplishment. I still think I could have helped his pronunciation and presentation of his speech. I shall always be glad to have associated with a student who leaped from *phooey* to *fractal* in two short years.

My first Asian student, however, came through a favorite custodian. Hung Lu (pronounced *Hoong Lu*) was a Vietnamese refugee. He was not bright; he was brilliant! Unfortunately, his tongue was slower than his brain, making him doubt his success in American education—especially higher education.

Knowing that I had special training for teaching English to foreigners, custodian Jake telephoned me to tell me about Hung's ambition. Jake said that he had been astonished how quickly and thoroughly Hung had worked in Central School District's summer program in maintenance. Jake gave Hung enough work to keep him busy for four hours. After an hour, Hung came to Jake and asked, "What I do now?"

Jake claimed that Hung was right: The work had been perfectly completed—and even better than Jake would have done working from eight o'clock in the morning until noon.

"But the kid doesn't think he can go to the U because he doesn't speak well enough. Would you help him?"

"Give him my telephone number and tell him to call me. If he really wants help in English, he will call," I replied.

Hung called. The following Saturday morning found me (after finding Hung's American family's home) teaching him for two hours the names and sounds of the American English alphabet and simple sentences. The next Saturday we spent two more hours doing the same thing, but with one of Hung's Vietnamese friends. As the summer Saturdays increased, so did the number of his friends.

One of the friends (a refugee like Hung) made his home with the family of the vice principal of one of Central School District's secondary schools, where most of the refugees were enrolled. The vice principal unlocked a math classroom every morning at 7:00 for six Vietnamese students. At 8:00, the school moved me to a study pod and kept me there until 3:30 or 4:00 in the afternoon. English and social studies teachers seemed pleased to send me not only Vietnamese, but also Spanish, Danish, Swedish, Japanese, Guamanian, Brazilian, Korean, and Filipino students—anyone difficult to understand, like Juan, who came and said, "Hab bansil?"

He wished for a pencil.

Chapter 15

High School Again

Hung Lu and Lam were from Vietnam. Both were placed by Lutheran Social Services with an American family in Central School District. Both were early refugees. They were not bright; they were *brilliant*. Hung was a superior thinker and reader of English, but his speech needed improvement. Lam came a school year later to the same family. His enunciation of words learned from his American parents and teachers was almost flawless. English words he had learned from Hung were scarcely recognizable.

One day when he arrived at 7:00 A.M. to our conference room in the library, he burst out with, "Da gurdo inna wocker neck to me, she say, 'How you doing?'

"I say 'Where?' She look at me funny and walk away. What I do wrong?"

"Oh, that's just another way of saying, 'How are you?'" I answered.

"I say, 'Fine'?" he asked.

"Yes, if you are fine. If you aren't, tell how you feel."

"What *fine* mean? I am here sin' May, this October. American parents tell me, 'Say *fine* if someone say, "How are you?" or "How do you do?" I say *Fine*. What *fine* mean?"

I knew he knew the meaning of the words *bad* and *good*, so I told him, "Fine is better than good."

"Oh," he said and seemed relieved. All would have been fine had I kept my big fat mouth shut. I didn't.

"Lam, the next time you see the girl in the locker next to you, ask her how she's doing."

The next session he asked immediately, "What's *cute*?"

I knew that 'the gurdo inna wocker neck to him' had told him he was cute.

Unwilling to go along with teenage slanguage (I should have known better), I dug into my briefcase and got out pictures before saying, "Babies, little children, and childlike women are cute."

"I not cute?" he said in desperation.

"No, Lam, you're not. You are good-looking."

"That mean I look good with my eyes?" His hands sought his face. His face was puzzled.

His American parents, teachers, and I all thought there must have been some French soldier in his ancestry. By Caucasian standards he was handsome, and I told him so.

"What's *handsome*?" he said as he raised both hands palm upwards.

He knew the words *pretty* and *beautiful* from previous reading, so I started like this, "What's the opposite of pretty?"

"Ugly."

"Right!" I said approvingly. "*Ugly, pretty—beautiful* we say for women. For men we say *ugly, good-looking—handsome*. You're handsome."

"I handsome?"

I nodded yes and smiled.

He smiled and said, "Thank you. Thank you *very* much."

One morning I feared and hated to start the third-level correlated reader, *Changes*, with my six Vietnamese boys. They ranged in age from fourteen to nineteen years old, according to my estimation. (In Vietnam a child is one year old the year it is born. Its first birthday, by their count, makes the child two years old because it is starting its second year.) What would my Vietnamese teenage boys think of a story of changes with a young couple about to have a baby?

In the story, the young husband grudgingly got a second job when the wife had to stop work because of the birth of the baby. The new father worked two weeks at two jobs before he got a day off. His wife was not pleased when the new father declared he was going fishing.

The *teacher's manual* suggested the teacher ask this question at this point of the story: "Which parent is right?" The boys didn't give me the chance to ask it. The order of their speeches is as follows:

"Whu matto wi him?" asked Number One.

"He cwazy," said Number Two.

"He stay home!" blurted Number Three.

"He hoda baby," Number Four said with authority.

"He owney liddo son," accusingly said Number Five.

"Whu matto wi him," repeated Number Six.

"*He cwazy!*" all six thundered in unison.

Silently, I thanked God that these young men were so family conscious and revered the nurturing of life. They had seen so much loss of life during the war and their escape from Vietnam. It was truly a refreshing experience for me to hear their contrasting ideas to what I had expected from thirty-five years of teaching American teenage boys.

💐   💐   💐

Horhay was an Asian student. He had chosen the name and its spelling because his parents operated a Mexican restaurant. The parents believed all Americans preferred Mexican food to their own delicious cuisine. His family had been in the States for five years. Maybe their first jobs had been Mexican restaurant work in a large city. Horhay's skin was similar to Mexicans' in color. He was more like the average fifteen-year-old American boy than like any of the other Asians. His idea of help for Driver's Education Class was for me to read the text and tell him the answers for each multiple-choice question for the next assignment. He had a rude awakening. He began to learn to read English.

One warm morning, Horhay started to sit in the chair to my right. It had been recently vacated by a student who had remained after the dismissal bell to ask some questions.

"Do I gotta sit in dis chair?" Horhay questioned as he immediately rose.

"No, you may have another chair, or sit on my left this morning," I answered.

He chose a completely different chair and, placing it to my right, he said, "I bet it was a girl with a fat hot butt," and he continued, "I hate girls with fat hot butts!"

I praised God that Horhay had not been with the six Vietnamese in *Changes*.

Before long Celest, an exchange student from Brazil, was sent to share second period with Horhay. It was the same period he struggled with the driver's ed test. Knowing Celest could read and write fairly well, I gave her a half-hour assignment and continued with Horhay.

It was a very short moment into Celest's English learning when the emotionally childish Horhay grabbed my arm and said, "Missus Souwar, whatza *burja* or *burjin*?"

"I really don't know, Horhay," I replied over my shoulder. "How was it used?"

"Dis guy he sings, 'My sweet, sweet burja or burjin'."

"There is a word *burgeon*, which means "begin to grow." Or, was the word *virgin*?"

"Ya, ya, dattsa word. What mean?"

Carefully I chose my words—not to offend my first-time meeting with Celest—and remembering it was 'dis guy' singing.

"It's a girl or young woman who has never been married," ventured I.

In the most disgusted tone imaginable, Celest loudly said, "It's anyone who hasn't had sex!"

🕊   🕊   🕊

There must be some belief in Asia that one should not sit in a hot seat. One noon, Binh Duong (called *Ben Dong* by Americans, but really *Bun Yong*) sat in another chair saying, "It's not good to sit on a hot seat, you know."

His English had improved considerably since the morning we read *Changes* two years prior. In that same sophomore year, he was required to give a speech or produce a project for world history class. He had very clever hands according to his shop teacher, and the man who provided his American home. There was a picture of a Shakespeare's Globe Theatre in his text (I think). I suggested he make one and explain it.

"No. I gonna tell about Greek 'tee-a-ter'" was his decision.

What trouble he had remembering his pronunciation of *orchestra*—a very necessary part of acted-out stories on the Greek stage. Every day for at least two weeks, and several times each hour of those sessions, he would say, "What's dat word?"

I would pronounce *orchestra*, spell it, pronounce it again, and demand that he would imitate what I had said. Finally, one day, pronouncing it for the ninth time, I explained for the umpty-ninth time the purpose of an orchestra. Then I did a very unprofessional thing.

"Binh, if you ask me one more time, I'm going to kick your butt. Do you understand?"

He nodded affirmative. He played both football and soccer, so I had a pretty good idea he knew what I meant.

"Where is it?" I demanded.

He patted his wallet in his back pocket and said "orchestra" perfectly for the very first time. It never gave him trouble thereafter.

Several years later, when he went to Australia, he sent me a photo of the marvelous futuristic theater in Sydney and under-lined the printed word *orchestra*.

After volunteering four years at the new high school, Central High called me back to teach—beginning at seven in the morning until noon—Mexican, Japanese, a Filipina, and many at-risk Americans besides Chinese, Argentineans, and a Russian.

Shortly after lunch (more times during), I left for one of the junior-high buildings where I would spend two hours and return either to Central or the new high school for after-school tutoring.

It was at the junior high that I found another brilliant Korean as a seventh grader. About the third week in October, his homeroom teacher telephoned me. She told me that she had a boy who had never answered roll since he began her class the first week in September. It was the same situation of not answering questions orally in class—except math class, if written figures were the only requirement. Collectively, the teachers began to think he was a deaf-mute. A Korean psychologist was not to be found.

October 20 I made sure to arrive early enough at that junior high so I could visit the office and learn two things: the boy's homeroom number and his name. I was wearing a plastic-covered nametag pin and had brought along an empty plastic pin, so I could print and insert his name in it. The office had him listed as Min Pak.

When I found his homeroom, his English teacher kindly led both of us to a glassed-in cubicle of the library. As soon as we were seated, I pointed to my name tag and gave him his. Looking at mine, he pinned on his immediately. I cupped my right hand behind my ear and placed my left index finger vertically in the middle of my closed lips. Laubach teachers have been told those movements are the signs of "Listen" and "Don't talk" in any language.

Then, pointing to my nametag, I said three times, "My name is Mrs. Southworth. What's yours?"

Next, I took his fingers and pointed to his nametag while saying, "My name is . . ." He finished with what sounded like "Mean Pock."

No wonder he had not answered roll in any class when all of his teachers said what sounded like *Min Pack*, not *Mean Pock*. He had a good ear and a good imitating tongue. He began with the sounds and names of the English alphabet, plus names of numbers that day.

By the end of January, he was reading third- and fourth-grade material in English. As soon as he learned the meaning of *mean* to be "ugly" and "cruel", he wanted to be called "Min Pock."

Bless his heart! One day in late November, he was in the library stacks. I had arrived an hour earlier to tutor a Filipino boy. Min came to the window of my cubicle. He was all smiles and raised his hand, palm toward me. In the middle of a wave, his face went straight and his hand dropped to his side. I never asked him, but I think he thought being friendly with a teacher was not the right thing to do—even in America.

He had changed by January of that same school year. One day he saw me and took hold of my sleeve and pulled me to the magazine rack in the junior-high library. Quickly, he pulled out a magazine featuring Judo. Not only did he wish me to read with him the article (He was already reading third-grade material), but he wanted me to demonstrate. Needless to say, despite my seventy-two years, I did. We both laughed. From then on we were friends.

Before school reached midterm of the second spring, Min's mother, Kumjah, wanted me to help her with English, too. That gracious lady showered me with gifts and invited Walt and me to their home. Kumjah had been an elementary schoolteacher in Korea. For our fiftieth wedding anniversary, she gave us a magnificent black-lacquered small chest inlaid with mother-of-pearl. The red, plush-lined box had an amazing likeness of us done in pencil. Min had copied and enlarged our picture from the newspaper. He was an excellent artist. His father remarked, "OK of teachuh. Very good of Grandfa."

★ ★ ★

Vicky was an exchange student from Brazil. One morning she was waiting for me in the library cubicle. Quickly, she shut the door and leaned against it.

"Am I pretty?" she asked.

In my estimation, her yellow, somewhat-crooked teeth and pockmarked skin would exempt her from a beauty pageant. As honestly as I could I said, "You have expressive eyes and nice curling eyelashes. You know how to wear your hair and makeup."

"Why I have no date for prom?" she interrupted.

Being a Scotch-Hebrew when it comes to money, I tried to explain that boys usually have a prom date with their steady girlfriends. Although I didn't actually know for sure, I assumed a prom date would cost about fifty dollars at that time. That amount included ticket, corsage, dinner, and transportation.

"Why don't you talk to Pedro? He, too, is a Latin-American exchange student here," I ventured.

"He's too short!" she quickly exclaimed.

Vicky was a tall girl, but I thought Pedro was taller. That very day I asked him his height.

"I theenk I'm seeks-feet-two and a leetle more," he said.

He was taller than Vicky, but she was definitely not interested.

"Why not ask Enrique, your friend from your hometown you met for the first time on the plane en route here? You exchange students should partake in as many US student activities as you can while here. Did you say Enrique attends one of the other high schools in the county?"

"I weel do dat," she concluded.

I breathed a sigh of relief. My matchmaking was done. I was wrong. The next Monday Vicky was all smiles and announced,

"Enrique won't come here, but he wants me to come da prom een heez school. We theenk eet will be fun."

As his prom was approximately a month after hers, I almost forgot to ask about the event after it happened. Vicky was a young woman of a few words. But her tone was specific, "Eeet wasn't wert feefty-dollar!"

Several years later when I was spending the whole day at Central instead of dividing my time between three schools, Vicky came back to visit her American family. She and her two- or three-years younger American brother found me in the library. Tony had brought her on his motorcycle. It was then they told me that he had taken her to Enrique's prom on his motorbike and waited for her someplace before taking her home. Her date didn't have transportation—not even a motorcycle. No wonder "Eeet wasn't wert feefty-dollar!"

🏵   🏵   🏵

Although Cam had seen me at Vietnamese parties hosted by Lutheran Social Services, he refused to let that organization arrange for me to tutor him. Then came the day I was called back to Central for a whole day, three days a week. At that time Cam was a sophomore struggling with, as he said, "We-road Hit-twee."

Having helped Binh Duong and two Guamanians pass world history at the new high school, it wasn't too difficult for Cam and me until the chapter following the Dark Ages. The two high schools did not have the same texts.

Both my high school and college texts in world history called that period The Order of Authority. That was not the title nor the content of Cam's text. His was more like a discussion on religions of the world. It began with a long discussion of the New Age. Then appeared more than a page on Islam, the same amount on Hinduism, slightly less on Buddhism, the same on Confucius and Taoism, plus Shintoism. About half a page was devoted to Judaism and less than two inches to Christianity.

After reading the chapter with Cam, I wrote what I remembered about the order of authority according to the Roman Catholic Church. I included God, the Pope, the Cardinals, Archbishops, Bishops, Friars, and Brothers—plus the schools and hospitals the monasteries and nunneries had developed.

The next day I came, Cam was bursting to tell me, "Yetter day I raise my han' for firt time in cwass. I say, 'Following the Dark Ages is da Order of Order.' Hittwee teacher tell me to expwain. I did. I say, 'Firt dere is Got, den da Peep or da Pop . . . I don't know how you say him, but you spell him capital *P-o-p-e*.'

"Kits say, 'How you know?

" I say, 'My teacher, Missy Jen Southwor' tell me.

"Then hittwee cwass teacher say, 'You are right, Cam. Did you know she was my teacher, too, when I was in high school here?' Den he wite on board all you say about Order of Order after da Peep or da Pop."

Late in the first quarter of his senior year, Cam telephoned me for help.

"Missy teacher, you say, 'I'm in twouble, you call me'."

"Cam, you know my name; say it."

"Missy Southworth, I in twouble. Ecology. Itta mess. Come please."

I did.

Chapter 16

Volunteer Office

Because of Cam, I was back in my favorite school—this time with an office, a chalkboard, and a desk. The other office desk was vacant. There were several straight-backed chairs.

"Are we glad to see *you!*" enthusiastically inflected the registrar. "We have a Mexican who doesn't speak a word of English. It is Roberto, who leaves school immediately at 2:30 to go to work at the Mexican Fiesta Restaurant."

She was not 100 percent right. The first time he pulled out my chair, he said, "Chair." It was the only word in English he knew. He had learned that word in the restaurant.

I was privileged to have Roberto for three years, two hours per day, three days a week. All that time he did his best. The first day the registrar or counselor called Roberto's US history teacher. That lady sent a junior boy out of her class to escort Roberto down to my office. Through lack of communication the school staff thought Roberto to be a junior. (All juniors take US History.) Instead he came from a Mexican junior high school. He was the middle child of a family of eleven children and had never seen snow. The second or third day the US history teacher sent him and his escort down, they were at least five minutes late. Snow had started to fall after school had begun. His escort had taken him out into the snow.

"Roberto was fascinated by the big fluffy flakes. He caught some. The first thing he did was try to taste one," said his escort as he closed my door and headed for his class.

"Do you like snow?" I asked.

"Cold," was all he could say.

As soon as he was able to find the tutoring office, he came promptly at 7:00 in the morning from his home before school started, as well as coming from third period US history class.

He was always on time except for snow in his senior year. That was the second time he was late because of snow. Roberto had driven to one of the larger cities on Puget Sound to visit his father. The older man was a chef in a Mexican restaurant. His father didn't want Roberto to drive on icy highways until they had been cleared and sanded.

In the spring, he missed nearly a week of school. That was most unusual. When he came back he proudly showed me a picture of him and "My wife, Susan, at her folks' place." Susan had graduated from Central the year before he did.

The next fall, Roberto spoke at the banquet for the Literacy Council, telling the diners that the only English word he knew before he met me was the word *chair*. When I called to learn their preference in meat, he was quick to say, "cheekin". His restaurant served a lot of beef.

We kept in touch for quite a while. The last I heard from Susan, they were living in New Mexico or Arizona, where Roberto had been accepted to an automotive school. She was so proud of his ability and confidence in English that he was not only able to register himself, but also to ask for the tools he would need at the store.

🜲 🜲 🜲

Another student from south of the border was Juan. He, too, had been enticed up here by the Fiesta Restaurant. It is doubtful if he had been in school in Mexico for more than two years. Because he was fifteen years old, the counselors had put him with tenth graders.

He did well in PE, but the PE teacher worried about his naive trust. He left his wallet in his jeans in his basket of the locker room. The PE teacher told me there was more than two hundred dollars in it one time. When Juan had saved two hundred fifty dollars, he sent that amount home. After he told me how much he earned, what his expenses were, and the amount he sent home, I wondered how many US citizens could expect that from their teenagers.

Juan's manuscript was quite good, as lettering goes. His cursive writing was nonexistent. Watching him print his name, I was sure my eyes weren't seeing correctly. He started at the tip of the curve, then went straight up to the top line. Forming the first letter, he lifted the pencil and made a cross bar like a capital *T* but moved from right to left. Each succeeding letter he made with movements from right to left also, starting at the bottom of each letter.

"That's backwards!" I said tactlessly.

"Wot means *bockwords*?" he asked rolling the *r*.

I rose and started toward the door, saying, "This is forward," as I walked. Then I backed up and continued, "This is backwards."

"Ladderss don't walk," he said.

Although I had taught the A. N. Palmer Method of Business Writing in the late 1930s, I was just learning to make the Laubach manuscript letters. Below his name I printed *J-u-a-n*, moving from left to right. Next, I intended to use a different colored pencil to show him how cursive was related to manuscript. He interrupted before I could change pencils, "Badder dan yourss!" he said proudly, holding up his printed name.

He was right.

🐛   🐛   🐛

One noon I turned left, bound for the cafeteria in the new east section of Central. (Actually that three-story section stands where I once threatened to wrap a dead snake around the necks of boys until one confessed.) There was a huge crowd of students at the top of what used to be the east stairwell. They were spectators to a fight. Two light-heavyweight wrestlers were fighting. Although they were on the floor, they were not wrestling. They were fighting. I forgot that it had been twelve years since I had been on the faculty at Central.

Snapping my fingers I barked, "That's enough!"

The unlimited heavyweight got up from squatting in the open doorway of the girls' lavatory and said with a sneer, "We'll see."

He flopped, stomach first, the length of the struggling bodies. His *derriere* was too tempting for me to resist. I slapped his right cheek with the full force of my right arm and hand as I commanded, "Knock it off!"

"Yes, mam!" responded the unlimited as he rose to tower over me.

"You go that way," I said pointing toward the science and math hall.

The two light-heavies got up and towered over me, too. Each said, "Yes, mam," and went the separate ways I pointed.

On the stairs below the landing, I wondered if by the time I reached the cafeteria I would be able to stir my coffee. My right hand was really stinging. Just then the principal met me. I stopped him.

"Sir, I confess my side of the story," and told him my part in what had just transpired and added, "You can't fire me. I'm a volunteer."

Placing a hand on each of my shoulders, and looking me straight in the eyes, he said, "Good for you! I wouldn't dare do that. *I'd* be fired."

Chapter 17

Failures

Have I had failures? Yes. Solomon says in chapter 16 of Proverbs, verse 18, "Pride goes before destruction and a haughty spirit before a fall." Grateful students and their families have lavished so many thanks, gifts, and praise on my tutoring that unconsciously I had begun to think that I could teach anyone. I forgot a very important thing: I can teach only if the student wants to learn.

Isobel came from Spain. She had a limp and two teenage girls. She loved to talk about them—and in that order. We met two times a week in the downtown library. It was hard holding her attention as the public walked in, out, and around.

Evidently she wanted a good job where she could sit, preferably as a cashier, but could not get one according to her, "Because I am physic." Her limp was a physical handicap.

For her second lesson she brought a hymnal. She wanted to know why the congregation didn't sing lines 1, 2, 3, and 4 as they were printed between the treble and bass clefs of the music.

Explaining that line 1 was the first line of a poem set to music to make it a song, I learned that Isobel loved poetry. Then it was easy for her to see the continuation of the verse on down the page.

As intensely as she loved poetry, she had two intense hates: Roman Catholics and men. She always desired a Christian tutor but no Catholic. Every Monday morning, she held forth a tirade on her husband and another male friend of his. The friend's drumming with his fingers on the back of his pew infuriated Isobel.

In fact, her idea of learning English was simply to spend each learning session reviling her husband and two teenage daughters, whom she referred to as her *dowries*.

Moving downstairs to the literacy-office kitchen helped. No matter which series of books the Literacy Council had to offer for beginning English, they weren't to her liking—all required homework.

For a short time I steered her clear of complaining about her dowries by asking her to bring her Spanish Bible. I brought one of my more recent versions. She made sure it was a Protestant Bible. Buying a Spanish-English dictionary and finding for her purchase a Spanish poetry book with English translation also helped for about three weeks. Then I searched for another series of reading and writing beginner's books. I had exhausted the Literacy Council's supply and everything I had, including the books that book salesmen had given me when I had taught reading improvement or when I headed the English Department at Central High School.

Finally, one morning I said, "Isobel, you have to do your homework in your *workbook*. You'll never learn to read and write English like this. You spend all the time talking bad about your family in poor English.

She rose and, in spite of her being "physic," limped straight to the literacy director and said, "Do I have to listen to Jen? She talk to me like a *man*!"

Both the Literacy Council and a member of a sponsoring church contacted me one summer to teach an Islamic family—father, mother, and a six-year-old son. The church was anxious for Baladan, the father, to become employable. That Iraqi gentleman was enrolled at the community college but attended rarely. My informant said that Baladan spoke a little English, but his wife spoke none. Possibly through Baladan's account that was not the case. It was the reverse.

Razina, the wife, met me at the door with Tahir, the six-year-old, who opened it for me. Razina held two-week-old Assad in her arms. Through smiles and gestures we sat on the daveno with the *Laubach Skill Book* I spread out on the coffee table. All three of us had covered page 2, the chart having the consonants *b* through *h*, when Baladan came home. He carried a six-pack of carbonated beverage in one hand and a half-gallon brick of ice cream in the other.

In good host fashion, Baladan's face and gestures invited me to have some. Being allergic to every component of ice cream, as well as the sugar in the soda, I shook my head negatively. But smiling while holding up my hands in a "stop" signal, I said, "No, thank you," as gently and firmly as I could.

Baladan put both refreshments in the refrigerator. Tahir jumped up and down, screaming in protest in the kitchen. Immediately Tariq awoke. That three-year-old child made his appearance jumping and screaming for the sheer joy of the activity. After about five minutes Tahir must have told his younger brother the situation because Tariq then angrily jumped and shrieked in earnest. Baladan said nothing; Razina said softly many times to no avail, "Please, Tariq."

Finally Tahir turned on the TV. Immediately Tariq grabbed the dial and turned it until no more stations were seen or heard. Then he did the reverse as far as the dial went in the opposite direction.

Because neither parent did anything, I opened my briefcase and handed Baladan his book. Tahir returned to the coffee table, and the three of them did the written work. Tiring of the TV, Tariq investigated my briefcase. As soon as he opened it he began unloading it. Again Razina said, "Please, Tariq."

The baby cried, and she began nursing little Assad. I managed to return the contents of the briefcase with some doubtful help from Tariq. But before I could lock it, he was tearing into it again. After many smiles from me, I managed to pat his little hands in a game fashion, close the top, and turn the locking dials. That brought on more jumps and screams.

Then Tahir got out a little electronic keyboard and plugged it in. Jumps and screams stopped. Tariq placed a fat little index finger on the next to the highest sounding key and held it there.

The high-pitched note must have gotten to Baladan, who had been writing in skill book 1. He got up quickly and pressed down on the low-volume control button. Then he slowly walked back the four or five feet to the end of the coffee table and sat down. As soon as he was seated, Tariq turned up the volume with his other chubby hand—never letting go of the next-to-the-last high key. This act was repeated again and again. Finally Baladan gave up. Tariq did not. My ears were worn out. I stood up and said, "I'm sorry, I'll have to go. I'll see you Saturday. Each of your books cost four dollars and fifty cents."

"No! No! In America everything is free!" Baladan yelled, rolling the r's in *America* and *free*.

Again I said, "I'm sorry. Everything in America is not free." I sat down to explain.

"I am free. You wanted me to teach all of you two hours per day, three days per week. That is easily worth thirty dollars an hour. I do not charge for my time."

"I don't need you. I go college," barked Baladan as he shoved his written-in workbook into my hands.

I started to say, "I'll be back . . ." when Tahir pushed me down by my shoulders to the sofa back, cracking my arthritic neck. That did it!

Snapping my fingers and pointing at him, I commanded, "Don't you dare interfere when I'm talking to your father!"

There was dead silence. Even little Assad quit making sucking noises. I put Baladan's book and my pencils into the briefcase and rose to go.

"I'll see you Saturday at 2:00."

Two days later, it was exactly 2:00 when I rapped on their door. Tahir opened it to reveal Razina. The look on her face told me that if she had not been encumbered with Assad in her arms and Tariq clinging to her knee, she would have embraced me. She and Tahir did well on lesson 2. The child lost interest in a little over thirty minutes. Not long after that, Tariq engaged Tahir in combat. Razina raised her voice in Arabic and vigorously snapped her fingers. The boys ceased. Maybe I had not taught much English the first day, but Razina learned something about American discipline.

When Baladan was home on Razina's tutoring days, he made himself scarce, unless he wanted me to read some mail or explain a bill or notice. He, too, made use of snapping his fingers at his two boys when they quarreled loudly.

About six weeks later, Razina fished a one dollar bill from an envelope on the wall. Tahir climbed on a chair and opened a cupboard from which he took a heavy, yellow plastic pitcher. It was more than half full of coins. Mother helped her son count out—in English—three more dollars and fifty cents in small change. Both beamed as I shook their hands, smiled, and said, "Thank you very, very much!"

Razina said the same words in English flawlessly as she patted Tahir's shoulder. He smiled proudly, held up the pitcher, and said, "My money!"

Razina was a very apt student. She had studied English in Iraq. Her sister was an English teacher near Babylon. Razina's understanding of printed English was amazingly good, but like most foreigners who study English in their own countries, she needed help with pronunciation. I admired her. She, her three children, and apartment were always spotless. She could nurse Asaad, snap her fingers to bring peace between her two older children, and never lose her place in the reading lesson. Her homework was always done and usually correct.

Razina telephoned me twice. Both calls were cancellations in adequate time. The first had to do with a trip to Canada. The trip lasted a week in the fall. The second one was for a doctor's appointment. In late fall they moved. Razina almost cried when I told her that my husband refused to drive me the ten or twelve miles to their new home. She said, "I understand."

After we had moved to a retirement community, several of my former high-school students sought help for their offspring. The children were not doing as well in school as their parents thought they should. Walt suggested that the parents thought if they had survived Mrs. Southworth, they would punish their children by bringing them to me. When I related that to a father of a little boy, he said with a laugh, "Or to get even with you."

The Lord has been very kind to me in letting me continue with my favorite activity—tutoring—for seventeen years. If my math has improved, that makes more than fifty years of teaching.

👑   👑   👑

Very recently the Lord blessed me with a lovely, young Japanese woman. Kanako had earned a degree in English literature at Hosei University in Japan. Her first words to me were, "I have a short beeza and I want conbersational Engrish."

Instead of a 180-day visa, she had been granted only ninety days. It was her desire to return to Japan to be a tour guide for English-speaking tourists to her country. She was already enrolled in a tutoring group with the Literacy Council and in an English as a Second Language Class at the community college in an adjoining town.

After trying unsuccessfully to teach her at the mall, we decided to move our learning sessions to my apartment. It was *much* quieter. I could hear her—most of the time. (One of my eighty-year-old ears doesn't function like it used to.)

Her second lesson revealed her confusion over a story assigned to her in either of the afore mentioned class or group. It was a story about two exconvicts. Both had gone straight. The character named Mr. Parsons evidently was more prosperous than the other former convict, who sold cigarette lighters for one buck each on the street.

Kanako had used her excellent English-Japanese dictionary. In the tiniest red letters I have been able to read, she had printed above the name Parsons, *Minister*. When we came to the last sentence of the first paragraph, which identified what the excon did for a living, she said, "I know light, lighter, and lightest, but how can one sell *lighter* for one *male animal*?"

She was such a joy to teach. Her desire to learn English, especially American idioms, was matched by her intelligence and persistence. Her letters to me are still prized.

❧ ❧ ❧

The fall semester of 1990 was a very busy time. I had ten or twelve students to teach at different times and different days. In addition, I had very foolishly agreed to be the coordinator of the Navy Math and Science Tutoring Program for Central High. It was my responsibility to arrange for after-school tutoring for high-school students by submariners and civilians working at another military base. That meant running all over each floor and section of the sprawling building. I acted as a messenger to connect tutors and students each Tuesday and Thursday for the two naval bases. It also entailed many calls to the base those days.

In November, my sister-in-law had major surgery. A large cancer was removed with between a third and a half of one of her lungs. The surgery also removed a rib. The only place for her recovery was our home. In December, a youngster with the lead for the Sunday school play chose me for the role of his grandmother. I couldn't say no.

Tuesday, December 18, was the second showing of our church's outdoor nativity in the evening. The Literacy Council's tea was early that afternoon. I felt I had to be at both. En route from the tea to the church, the temperature dropped. Suddenly the rain turned to snow. Big fluffy flakes covered the icy roads. They were treacherous, especially Hill Road. The weather cancelled the outdoor nativity. Walt insisted I leave the Jeep at the church and ride home with him in his four-wheel-drive Honda. It took us a little over two hours to drive those five miles. All employees from the three big military installations and all the schools were trying to get home simultaneously.

Everything came to a white—or black—halt for four days. Electricity was off and so were many telephones. If pumps depended on electricity, there was no fresh water in the house. Praise the

Lord for the fireplace! We slept in sleeping bags in the living room; we took off only our shoes. The next day, Walt loaded the porch with firewood and dug out some long-forgotten lignite coal. The frozen steps, porch, and living room were a mess after four days.

According to pre-Thanksgiving plans, the Southworth clan arrived at our dirty house for the annual Christmas party the Saturday before Christmas. Counting Southworth in-laws, outlaws, grandchildren, and great-grandchildren, more than twenty people crowded around the Christmas tree hidden behind all the packages. Christmas was the next day, and four close family members came again for dinner.

My cheeks didn't need rouge. They burned all afternoon. I thought they were hot because I had roasted a brace of ducks in the oven. Our dinner was late. (The cook dragged her feet.) More than eight extra-strength Tylenols had failed to quell my headache.

The alarm clock rang at 5:45 the next morning. A doctor had given me an early appointment. I punched Walt with my elbow as I turned off the alarm and thought I was going to say, "It's time to get up."

I did not, but said, "Kittum, kittum, kittum," and burst out laughing.

Walt thought he should take me to an insane asylum. I could not tell him why I laughed. Immediately thoughts of Lottie and her mother had come to mind. What came out of my mouth sounded so much like Lottie's:

May-ee kit-tum due'm boy
Ee ish you di wi deepum joe.

That ministroke, really a TIA (transient ischemic attack) put me in the University of Washington Medical Center for four days. Because the weatherman predicted another snowstorm, the doctors dismissed me early. The Honda drove into our carport just as the storm hit. God really takes care of his own!

Chapter 18

Apples for the Teacher

Teachers hope to make a difference by influencing and inspiring their students. As you have read in this book, know that I was uncertain how others saw my teaching and disciplinary practices. I did the best I knew how but always thought that I might be wrong.

At the start of these memory recordings, I couldn't recall every humorous incident that occurred through the last fifty years with over five thousand students. Most of them whom I asked responded, "Anything funny in *your* class? You must be kidding!"

Annette Philippson Churbuck said, "This maybe sounds funny, but we kids knew beneath that stainless steel armor of yours there was a little warm heart."

My typist—herself a former student—wrote to several former Central students and asked if they remembered any humorous incidents. I was disappointed in what came back. Not memories of high jinx, but memories of Mrs. Southworth as a teacher who made a difference in their lives. I was astounded!

Their answers comprised the greatest reward a teacher can receive. They are an inspiration to anyone in the teaching profession. Therefore, I am letting Paula include excerpts from the letters as a tribute to their authors. "Thank you from the bottom of my heart! Your letters attest I must have done something right after all."

Dear Mrs. Southworth:

Many memories of my best and favorite teacher return when talking to others. Two, however, stay with me:

"Jenny says pass" ("I don't know")—your response to your French professor. A delightful example then that even teachers are human!

The second, not so pleasurable, is the pain of your reaction to the stress of play productions. Your arms, wrists to elbows, would erupt in a rash that was excruciatingly itchy and painful. You would keep it covered with bandages and occasional cold-water rinses in the restroom. Ah—too many years before cortisone cream! I do hope that ailment passed, but I doubt you ever became relaxed with a production.

Perhaps a third memory: your requirement of students that they *learn* and try for excellence. Sometimes you did it with patience and sometimes with fear—but always with the goal in sight.

—*Juanita McAnnally Settine*

Dear Paula:

In your letter you mentioned our former teacher, Jen Southworth. I remember her vividly. She made literature come alive for me. I thought she was an outstanding teacher. Her classes were some of the best classes I ever had, and she is a great teacher! She made her classes *so* interesting.

I cut out an article—either from *AARP* magazine or *Friendly Exchange*. It was about Mrs. Southworth's teaching career and, after retirement, her work as a tutor—still helping people learn. A wonderful article about a *wonderful* teacher.

It must be a wonderful experience to be typing the pages of her book. That book should be very interesting. She had such insights into the *nature* of her students . . . a very understanding person. It was reflected in her students' esteem for her in return.

—*Charlene Cribb Grayson*

Jen,
 The only thing about the past that comes to mind, you may already remember. When we were trying to keep the *This Is Your Life* celebration for you secret, and we needed to tell everyone to come backstage for it, but you were onstage so we had to get you out. Anyway, I told Paul Mastel to get you off stage somehow. He did!
 "Come back here quick! Someone's barfing!"
 So you went. We made the announcement, and it all somehow worked out. What a night!

*   —Ann Sperber Almond*

Dear Mrs. Southworth,
 You didn't know how much I hated school and you were my only hope as a teacher, leader, and Christian.
 Your confidence helped me to be strong and grow. You'll never know the times when life has tried to conquer me that I would think of you reaching up to write—(with straight penmanship). I know that sounds funny, but I always thought that was so wonderful that you took the time to set an example of your penmanship. You probably never knew your penmanship gave me courage. I would think of you and your stories like *Little House on the Prairie*. (I do hope those stories are in your book.)
 All the things you went through, you never stopped trying. All the things I went through I would think, if this little short person can overcome anything, surely I can. But first I knew your strength: God.
 I always remembered you giving everyone a chance and trusting them until they proved themselves wrong. That's been one of my mottos ever since and, of course, has enriched my life with several friends.
 I learned my main purpose in life was to encourage people, and you were one of the main inspirations of that.
 I want you to know how grateful I am God put you in my life. Thank you for your sacrifices, time, effort, love, hugs, and help.

*   —Ginger Balter Minus*

Dear Mrs. Southworth,
 -While in one of your classes, possibly sophomore literature, I was seated near a very talkative Bert Olsen. Also in the same general area was an equally talkative Jim Turner. After several requests that

Bert cease talking, I heard this *swoosh* pass between his desk and mine in the adjacent row. It was a ring of keys that would have put any custodian to shame and drop a horse.

To this day, I don't know if your throwing ability was that good or it was Bert's lucky day. Needless to say, there was silence.

I somehow doubt this will make it into your book, but it is one memory I have. I have many more positive memories of you as a teacher and I am grateful to have been one of your many students.

—*Jeanie Ross Harrison*

Paula,

I don't have many memories to send Jen, as I was one of those gals that got married and never made it to her class. I know she remembers the Tonge clan, but probably associating me with brothers and sister and classmates.

Although I never experienced the pleasure of learning from this great lady, I did experience the comfort of her caring as we stood hand in hand and prayed for the return of my grandson to my son.

Wouldn't it be wonderful to have touched and had positive experiences on others as Mrs. Southworth has and still does?

—*Fran Tonge Starrett*

Dear Mrs. Southworth,

I wish I could think of something humorous that happened in school or Thespians. I'm sure there were hilarious moments. But these aren't the moments I remember. The memories I have are those of significant growth in myself; times when I was challenged to take a risk by auditioning for a part or directing a one-act play; times when we were all guided with a firm hand from frivolous teenage giggling to responsibility and quality of performance on stage. You molded character. You instilled a code of conduct that I still follow today with my students. You did this with steel, humor, and love.

Certainly, there were many special little moments: The time you searched for some jobs for me to do so I could earn those few more Thespian points that I needed. The time you grabbed me and gave me a big hug and said when you liked someone you liked to hug them. It's been almost thirty years and I still remember how important that hug was to me.

The most important things I gained can't be measured or adequately expressed. I found self discipline, a great feeling of worth, and that all of us need that hug. These things are important only to me, but imagine all of the other *hundreds* of people who feel the same way I do. The ripple effect is powerful, and hopefully many of us are creating ripples ourselves.

—*Marcia Holt*

Mrs. Southworth,

Memories . . . The opportunity to spend time at the University of Washington to visit a production on *Show Boat.*

There are so many special memories of our productions at CH. The comradery and the responsibility learned. In Psych class, it was early and often cold, but you kept the windows open. No sleeping in your class.

I learned things were not what they appeared to be. You shared about being asked to give a recommendation for someone who had raised many problems while in school, and after much thought you said he had leadership abilities. That there is something positive about everyone, even when leading in the wrong direction.

I'll never forget your sharing about two girls sending in for information on how to increase bust size and were sent a picture of a man's hand.

I played Magda in a one-act play, *Joseph Comes Home behind the Iron Curtain.* My husband was taken to prison. With much jubilation the family anticipated his return. They brought him home in a shoebox. I screamed. In the critique, you said it would have had much more impact had I had stunned silence.

You were highly respected. We always knew where you stood. Thanks for being strong and consistent.

—*Colleen Langill Mey*

Dear Mrs. Southworth,

Thank you! That is the basic message that I wanted to deliver. The *Harbrace College Handbook* you presented in your Honors English class on very nearly a daily basis was a gift whose value only became apparent years after the giving, and I appreciate it.

That gift, useful as it is, pales in comparison to the far greater benefits that I have realized from your influence. I enjoyed reading the literature, and the discussions in class were great. But the largest and most lasting benefit came from the research paper that you required us to write. Many of us shared the same reaction to your recitation of the required numbers of source documents and length of the finished product: "I can't do that!"

Fortunately, that initial reaction was not permanent. Your patient teaching of a systematic approach to breaking a huge, seemingly impossible project into small achievable tasks cured it. It has also carried over to many areas far beyond the writing of research papers. None of my college courses, in two-year or four-year institutions, ever required a research paper with anywhere near the number of sources or length of the one that I prepared for your class.

The analogy about breaking the mold certainly applies to you, especially in these days of outcome-based education and awards of self-esteem without accomplishment.

Thanks again.

—*Mike Moore, class of '67*
Business Manager
Dieringer School District

PS: I know, postscripts may not be proper, but I am compelled to add this. I have also never chewed gum in a classroom since holding it to the blackboard with my nose in front of your class for what seemed like hours.*

---

* AUTHOR'S NOTE: Today I would be fired for cruel and unusual punishment.

To order additional copies of

send $10.99 plus $3.95 shipping and handling to

Books, Etc.
PO Box 1406
Mukilteo, WA 98275

or have your credit card ready and call

(800) 917-BOOK